Literacy and Education

Literacy and Education

Understanding the New Literacy Studies in the Classroom

KATE PAHL AND JENNIFER ROWSELL

P·C·P

Paul Chapman
Publishing

Paul Chapman Publishing
A SAGE Publications Company
1 Oliver's Yard
55 City Road
London EC1Y 1SP

SAGE Publications Inc
2455 Teller Road
Thousand Oaks, California 91320

SAGE Publications India Pvt Ltd
B-42, Panchsheel Enclave
Post Box 4109
New Delhi 110 017

Library of Congress Control Number: 2004096886

A catalogue record for this book is available from the British Library

ISBN-10 1-4129-0113-8   ISBN-13 978-1-4129-0113-0
ISBN-10 1-4129-0114-6   ISBN-13 978-1-4129-0114-7 (pbk)

Typeset by Pantek Arts Ltd, Maidstone, Kent
Printed in Great Britain by T.J. International, Padstow, Cornwall

This book is dedicated to our mothers:

Jan Pahl
and in memory of Sunny Rowsell

Contents

Foreword

Literacy and Education is a comprehensive introduction to social and cultural approaches to literacy specifically written for teachers and teacher educators. This book brings together the diversity of approaches, research and findings of work in the field. For those currently teaching, it will provoke your thinking and unsettle your practice. The book makes a compelling case for rethinking what we do with new media cultures, with globalized flows of information and text, how we engage students' diverse backgrounds and understandings of the world. For those of you who are training to become teachers, Kate Pahl and Jennifer Rowsell have drawn upon their years of experience as teachers, teacher educators and researchers across several countries to provide useful narratives, illustrations and texts from children's lives and work.

There is a history behind the work that is drawn together here. It is worth recounting this not because it is particularly heroic, but because it offers key lessons on what literacy education, schooling and teaching are really about, how they change and why, and the ethical decisions facing teachers. Stable moments in literacy education are few and far between. Agreement in public and professional debates about how best to introduce children to reading and writing, viewing and surfing the Web is rare. This is not because the field has not arrived at a definitive scientific answer from field trials, laboratory work or experimental design, as the current UK and US policy debates would lead us to believe. The reason is that how we 'make' and 'shape' what students do with texts and discourses – how we 'construct' literacy and literate students – is utterly dependent not on some science of literacy, but upon how literacy figures and refigures in the changing economies, cultures, institutions and possible worlds that we inhabit.

Literacy is a malleable repertoire of practices, not an unchanging or universal set of skills. Learning to be literate is like learning to be an artisan in a guild, to play an instrument in an ensemble, like acquiring a craft within a community whose art and forms of life are dynamic, rather than a robotic acquisition and automization of core skills. Once we understand this, Pahl and Rowsell's approach suggests, we can find the resources, grounds and normative purposes for teaching literacy not from textbooks and skill taxonomies, but by attending closely to what children and communities actually do with texts, old and new, print and multimodal, traditional and radical. This requires something more than common sense, and that we get out of the staffroom, get away from the teachers' guidebooks and draw upon all our skills as teacher intellectuals, as psychologists and sociologists, linguists and ethnographers. According to *Literacy and Education*, the systematic engagement with these everyday texts, discourses and practices is at the heart of teaching and learning. And it is in these artefacts and practices – like those of the children you meet here – that you will find the generative domains, texts and practices for lessons, units and classroom events.

Thirty years ago, when many teachers and researchers embarked on the rich interpretive work described in *Literacy and Education*, we were told it could not be done. Fields like 'new literacy studies' or 'critical literacies' or 'multiliteracies' did not exist. Paulo Freire was a fringe and suitably dangerous figure in North American literacy education circles, rarely surfacing in teacher education programmes. Moving out from our own work as teachers, as activists and artists, as cultural 'minorities', into the graduate programmes of education faculties across Canada, Australia, the UK and the USA, we often were told simply and directly to be quiet and study traditional reading psychology, then making its historical shift from behaviourism to cognitive and psycholinguistic models. It was in the move from 'decoding' to 'comprehension', from behaviour to a cognitive psychology of language, our mentors and supervisors explained, where the new breakthroughs for the improvement of schools would be found, where the great work has to be done. Fair enough. Paradigms gained and lost. But such stories are always far more complex in their detail, and far more simple in their force, than they appear.

Change in the social sciences were marked by what is called the 'linguistic turn' that began in the 1960s and the 'discourse turn' of the 1980s. Each had its legacy for educators and schools. We would not be focusing on the links between children's language and cognition, on their home–school transitions, on the complexities of their multilingual resources, and on how schools, societies and media influence these, were it not for this work.

Sitting underneath the educational studies cited in this book you will find foundational claims by Noam Chomsky, Dell Hymes and Michael Halliday, but also those of Michele Foucault and Jacques Derrida. But to assume it was the 'truths' of emergent sciences of psycholinguistics and sociolinguistics, cognitive science and French discourse theory that set the grounds for the new literacy studies would be, at best, a partial if not erroneous conclusion.

Change in literacy education is about change in the material worlds of social life and practice. And it is the new lived experiences and histories of childhood, work and leisure that are the real educational challenges of this millennium – not phonics or scripted reading programmes.

This is a period of profound cultural and demographic, social and political transition. Schools and education systems, teacher education programmes and research are struggling to keep up. The schools where we were taught and learned to teach were geared up for monocultural, print children; they were designed to service stable post-war industrial economies, to reproduce relatively static and stable disciplinary knowledge, and to cultivate 'local' and often narrowly parochial identities and national ideologies. From weekly spelling study to multiple choice, fill-in-the-blanks worksheets, from show-and-tell to handwriting exercises, the pedagogical routines of the 1950s' primary school have proven remarkably durable and resistant. But while we debate which of these texts and practices are of continuing educational value, the identities, histories and resources of our students have changed.

The children described in Kate Pahl's ethnographic studies of growing up with media, popular culture and creative play cannot be explained away simply by reference to their obstensive 'migrant multiculturalism' or 'linguistic diversity'. The issue is not one where 'deficit'-based approaches can be redressed via more English as a Second Language programmes and celebration of multiculturalism days. So many of the studies reviewed here paint a far more complex picture. Increasingly more children in post-industrial economies grow up in saturation multimodal information environments, from a very early age engaged by television, video games, popular music, print media, the Internet and a 'consuming' culture of powerful images and messages. These in turn mediate and shape linguistic competence, but also 'ways of taking' from the environment, ways of manipulating symbol systems, ways of playing and making sense, senses of self and the communicative norms with which they conduct and manage their relations with others. In one sense, this is not news: children, childhood and language socialization are by definition multi-semiotic, blending image, speech and sound, music and embodied gesture and, later, more formal systems of writing and inscription. But current conditions have opened up new modalities for communication and new forms of knowledge, many of which are 'high stakes' in the building of social position and power, and in the navigation of life pathways and destinations. In conditions of 'fast capitalism', contexts and flows shift with great speed and rapidity, such that the actual images and practices of childhood and everyday life appear to be in perpetual motion. This requires something more than educational explanations based on models of 'cultural diversity' or 'multilingualism'. For teachers now have to deal with a species of *epistemological diversity*, where students bring to classrooms complex, multiple and blended background knowledges, identities and discourses, constructing identity and practice from a range of scripts that go far beyond the 'two worlds' metaphors of multicultural education.

Whether we can call it the 'post' or the 'post-post-war', or for the most apocalyptic and cynical 'clashes of civilization', and the 'end of history', it is not surprising that the response of many educators, communities and parents to globalized economies, polyglot cultures and mass-mediated childhoods is a kind of educational fundamentalism (Luke, in press): a reductionist call for a simpler, more literal and slower approach to literacy, and as well, to childhood, to education and to growing up. But to dismiss new domains of literacy out of hand or to treat them as historical aberrations likely to 'go away', would be to abrogate our responsibilities as educators.

For its part, *Literacy and Education* sets the ground for a critical engagement with these new cultures and new worlds, for teachers and teacher educators to literally move from a reactive stance to a more dynamic engagement with these changes. Such an engagement does not necessarily mean sanctioning new families of practices, but focuses on exploring the potential for what the New London Group (1996) termed 'critical and transformed practice'. Across the work of the 'New Literacy Studies' is one generational, cultural and ultimately political response: an abiding commitment to literacy as a means of social transformation – for individuals and communities, for cultures and nation-states. These range from commitments to education as a force for a more equitable redistribution of social goods, power and capital, to a commitment to literacy education as a 'practice of freedom' as Freire (1972) argued three decades ago.

As teachers and educators, we have heard all the standard arguments about why one cannot do the 'critical', the 'social' and even the 'cultural' in literacy education: that there will be insufficient provision of basic decoding skills; that teachers do not have the requisite skill and knowledge itself; that the state and its 'official knowledge' do not allow it; that parents will object; that the kids are not developmentally capable enough; that this talk about 'critical literacy', 'critical multiculturalism', 'media studies' and multimodality is all theoretical and not practical. Kate Pahl and Jennifer Rowsell here offer a resounding response to such claims.

The assumption often underlying educational paradigm shifts is that they begin and end from breakthrough works. There is indeed now a 'canon' of works on social, cultural and political approaches to literacy that Pahl and Rowsell here bring together with great care and fidelity – mixing recent work by new scholars in the field with their own insightful work with kids and teachers in Canada and the UK.

But regardless of where it begins, the reframing of an educational field like literacy does not lead to an epic work. It leads us right back to where it should: the everyday domains of classrooms, teacher training programmes, homes, where teachers, parents and 'world kids' do the work of representation and discourse-making, of culture and development, of capital, communication and exchange. Real paradigm change reshapes our everyday practice and common sense. And *Literacy and Education* is a powerful introductory resource for doing just that: changing the ways that we teach and learn.

Allan Luke
Jurong, Singapore
September 2004

REFERENCES

Freire, P. (1972) *Education for Critical Conciousness*. New York: Seabury Press.

Luke, A. (in press) 'Literacy and educational fundamentalism: an interview', *English Quarterly*, 36(4).

New London Group (1996) 'A pedagogy of multiliteracies: designing social futures', *Harvard Educational Review*, 66(1), 60–92.

About the Authors

Jim Cummins teaches in the Department of Curriculum, Teaching and Learning of the Ontario Institute for Studies in Education of the University of Toronto. His research has focused on the nature of language proficiency and second language acquisition, with particular emphasis on the social and educational barriers that limit academic success for culturally diverse students. His current interests include identifying pedagogical options for supporting literacy development for critical social participation. His publication include *Language, Power and Pedagogy: Bilingual Children in the Crossfire* (Multilingual Matters, 2000).

Allan Luke has taught and done research in Canada, the US, Australia and Singapore. His current work at Nanyang Technological University, Singapore, studies new forms of Asian pedagogy, identity and capital in the context of globalization, rapid economic shift, and changes in East Asian nation states.

Kate Pahl is a Lecturer in Education at the University of Sheffield. Her work has included a study of children's meaning making in a nursery – *Transformations: Children's Meaning Making in a Nursery* (Trentham, 1999) – and she has written on literacy practices in homes and communities. She is particularly interested in children's literacy and popular culture, and has published on children's textual explorations of console games in home settings. Her work focuses on family and community literacy, and she has conducted a number of evaluations of family literacy provision in the UK.

Jennifer Rowsell teaches language and literacy education in the Bachelor of Education and graduate programmes at the Ontario Institute for Studies in Education (OISE) of the University of Toronto. Her research focuses on applying New Literacy Studies and multiliteracies in the classroom; multi-modality in children's meaning-making; and the role of new media in literacy education.

Acknowledgements

Kate and Jennifer both wish to thank: Lynda Graham, Anne Michelle Burke, Hilary Janks and Brian Street.

Kate wishes to acknowledge: Sally Kelly, Clair Marsh, Veronica Storey, Musseret Anwar, Croydon Education and Training Service (CETS); Carol Taylor, Karen Hanson, Read on Write Away! Derbyshire; Val Petersen and the English on-line team at The Sheffield College; Nora Hughes, Institute of Education; Pamela Greenhough, Graduate School of Education, University of Bristol; Eve Bearne and Henrietta Dombey, United Kingdom Literacy Association; Viv Bird, The National Literacy Trust. I would like to thank my colleagues at the School of Education, University of Sheffield, in particular: Julia Davies, Jackie Marsh, Elaine Millard, Jon Nixon, Peter Hannon and Greg Brooks, for their support and encouragement.

Jennifer wishes to acknowledge: Sandra Cheng, Robyn Cunningham, Angela Comia, Marianna Diiorio, Brenda Stein Dsaldov, Rita Gravina, My-Linh Hang, Simon Ives, Chi-Binh Lam, Lisa McNeill, Steve Pirso, Carrie Szu and Andras Valezy for their expertise, guidance and classroom moments. I would like to thank my colleagues at OISE/University of Toronto for their support and suggestions, in particular, Clive Beck, David Booth, Clare Kosnik, Shelley Peterson and Larry Swartz. A special tribute goes to Lois Gatt for her inspired teaching.

INTRODUCTION:

Taking Account of the Local

Why did we write this book? For too long, teachers have been at the mercy of government programmes which have emphasized the acquisition of literacy as a set of skills. In the UK, the National Literacy Strategy has stressed the importance of phonics-based, set programmes for the acquisition of literacy skills by children. In the USA, increasing focus from *No Child Left Behind* (2002) on drill and skills-based literacy has been instrumental in delivering a certain conception of literacy.

In this book, we dare to think otherwise. We want to suggest that exciting new theory coming out of the New Literacy Studies actually helps our students to access literacy skills. However, it comes to literacy with a different premise. What if, instead of assuming that our students are not engaging with literacy outside school, we bring our students' literacy practices into the classroom? What would happen then?

This book is an attempt to bridge the gap between theory and practice. Drawing on our experiences of literacy studies from either sides of the Atlantic, we knit together the rich research tradition which has studied out of school literacy, the complex third spaces of childhood and young adulthood, into the more regimented classroom spaces.

Who is this book for? This book is for teachers who work with young children, teenagers or families who wish to explore how they can engage with their students through literacy. By thinking about the literacy practices of our students, we argue, a richer and more satisfying curricula can be developed.

We argue that by acknowledging our students' identities in their literacy practices, we can come to support and sustain their engagement with schooling. When we write, text, email or tell stories, we inscribe into these practices our identities. In this book identity comes to the fore as something that is inscribed into literacy practices. By giving our students' literacy practices recognition within classrooms, we let in identities.

In this book, we combined theory with practice. In order to illustrate our message, we have gathered examples of practice from Toronto, London, Croydon, Sheffield, Derbyshire and Newfoundland, drawing on combined experience of working in the field of literacy, both in and out of schools, in after-school programmes, family literacy classes, and primary and secondary school classrooms. We have a shared interest in our students, in their narratives of migration, of loss or displacement and the artefacts they use to describe these narratives.

To that end, we take our readers on a journey. We start with the New Literacy Studies and what it offers the teacher. Chapter 1 considers how the concept of literacy practices supports classroom teachers. Chapter 2 takes account of the theories of multimodality and visual communication, which are current, and are beginning to be inscribed into teaching (QCA, 2004). Chapter 3 moves into an account of home–school and how our students' home literacy practices can be taken up within classrooms. Chapter 4 moves into the wider globalized world we share, and considers how the local and global interact in classroom literacies. Chapter 5 considers identity, and its role in shaping literacy. Chapter 6 explores how curriculum and pedagogy can be shaped by the ideas of the New Literacy Studies.

By linking theory and practice, we hope to offer literacy teachers an inspiration that they can become active researchers of their students' literacy practices. We argue that this works. Studies both in the USA, the UK and worldwide have recognized that by 'taking account of the local' students' literacy skills are enhanced (Condelli, 2003; Street, personal communication, 2004). Government initiatives that rely solely on assessment and testing regimes are beginning to ask about the other ways in which literacy skills can be improved. Increasingly, governments are recognizing that for civic participation to take place, the literacy skills of communities need supporting. In the UK, community-focused literacy initiatives have begun to look at how schools, libraries, museums, early years centres and other community organizations, can work together to improve literacy across all ages. These community-wide literacy initiatives offer the promise of a new kind of literacy curricula which puts communities at the heart of literacy.

But in order to do this, we need to take account of the local: to consider how children engage with literacy in their homes; how adults engage with literacy in their daily lives. As communities grapple with the immense changes of the Internet and the World Wide Web, they inscribe these new practices into their daily routines, and move on to new, globalized literacy practices. The global and the local work in a dialogic relationship with each other, each speaking to another. How can we take on these challenging new communicative forms, and work them to our advantage, as teachers? This is what this book is for, and we hope it begins to answer the question of why it matters that we do take account of the local.

WHY LITERACY AS A SOCIAL PRACTICE?

Or, why do we need to revise our view of literacy? To begin with, there is a clear gap between the way we are teaching reading and writing in school and the sophisticated set of practices students use outside school. Covering language as a skill in the curriculum speaks to a fraction of the skills children actually need to make meaning in the world. Literacy is not a neutral set of skills that we have in our heads and develop through language teaching and learning. Rather, literacy is always and everywhere situated and, what is more, literacy is inseparable from practices. Traditionally, literacy has been regarded as being competent with printed texts – whether that is reading them or writing them. Brian Street defined an autonomous model of literacy as a neutral technology that can be used in different contexts and for different purposes to complete a set of tasks. In different parts of the world and even districts within our immediate context, literacy teaching is still taught within an autonomous model (Street, 1993).

In the 1970s and 1980s, this rather limited notion of literacy was expanded to take account of sociocultural influences. The term **literacies** emerged to signal the different ways people use language. Literacies come in association with practical purposes. Clearly, language use is tied to larger practices: learning how to read in primary school; playing *Super Mario* with friends; reading a recipe. Literacy as decoding and encoding without consideration of context belies the complex nature of reading and writing.

When we read and write, we are always doing it in a certain place for a certain purpose. In Chapter 1, we open up our notion of literacy by breaking apart the act of reading and writing. By defining, illustrating and making sense of literacy practices and literacy events, we consider the fluidity of language use. Context, identity and practice are three key terms central to any reading and writing event – in school or out of school. We present theorists who have challenged the traditional phonics, whole language and, even, balanced literacy models of literacy to confront head-on the way we regard literacy. To illustrate what we mean, we provide vignettes of teachers in different contexts engaging in meaningful language moments very much tied to the New Literacy Studies paradigm. Finally, we look at the implications of introducing these new theories into our teaching.

WHY MULTIMODALITY AND MULTILITERACIES AS FRAMEWORKS FOR LANGUAGE TEACHING?

Or, why should we look beyond the linguistic to other aspects of language use? A crucial factor in our public, professional and academic debate over how to teach literacy is the prevalence of technology in our communication systems. We know that not everybody has access to a computer. However, we have reached a point in our language teaching when most students think in terms of technology. This renders problematic the view of language that is used in most literacy curricula around the world. When we speak of technology, we are not focusing solely on technical skills like clicking, cutting and pasting, but instead on the cultural and critical ramifications of technology. Students should view texts they use inside and outside school as related to contexts. They are made up of different kinds of modes – written, visual, audio. Texts carry traces of the way they were put together. Students will not be able to explore this view of reading and writing if they are taught language in isolation from reading schemes.

Gunther Kress and others have argued that at some point very soon our primary vehicle for communication, and, more significantly, language use, will be governed by the screen. What this means for our students is that they will understand language use within an electronic medium. Language is not, and clearly will not be, printed texts with incidental images, but instead texts of all kinds with colour, different fonts, on monitors or mobile phones with sound, gesture and movement.

In Chapters 2 and 4 we discuss how we can prepare our classrooms for this new communicational frontier and we offer different ways of thinking about the literacy curriculum. There are many teachers around the world who already adopt many of the principles of a multimodal and multiliterate approach to teaching literacy. We offer vignettes of various educators who open up language to incorporate different modalities. In addition, we discuss how to teach in a way that takes account of the different languages our students speak.

WHY DO WE NEED HOME–SCHOOL TIES?

Or, why do we teach literacy as a community practice? What lies beneath the surface of the book is a belief that literacy is tied to students' cultural backgrounds. What this entails is a tie to belief systems, languages, values, goals and technical skills. Literacy is also tied to community values and groups. It links people to each other and to their shared histories. Letters written decades ago can become artefacts of identity, to be returned to and re-read. Books and personal artefacts are tied to our changing sense of who we are in the world. Our students carry around tool kits which make up who they are and literacy is tied into that. Literacy is tied to democratic practices and social emancipation. Whether expressed as a piece of graffiti, a child's letter to a friend or an adult's practice of recording thoughts in a diary, literacy supports identity, and travels through our lives with us. Within literate practices our lives are inscribed. We leave traces of literate practices as we move through life, either on our email or in the form of notes, postcards and other communicative practices such as photographs. This weaves our lives together in talk and stories. This view of literacy, as inscribed meaning, moving traces of identity, is the one we take forward in this book. Literacy reminds us of who we are, and gives us our friends, even if they are absent. It is the past and the future, rolled up into a continual text.

Children enter this world of literacy and immediately engage with it. They watch us as we engage with daily life. In Chapter 3 we look at language learning not as something that begins once a child enters the classroom and gets a language notebook and concludes at the end of the school day. Rather, we present language learning as taking place during every waking moment of our lives. By moving across contexts, we are actively between and among language systems. When we are at home we speak and act in a way that is different from school. As literacy educators, we need to build and access this language in our teaching. Anyone who has witnessed a group of boys using gamecards will know that they have an impressive repository of words and vocabulary that is not often tapped into. When they are engaging in a literacy event at school like a literature circle, or a guided reading session, they may be underachieving, but when they are put in front of a book or videogame that they love, you are presented with a very different language learner.

A critical piece in teaching literacy lies in the socially constructed nature of human practices and meaning-making systems. Language is used to construct an identity for ourselves within a speech community. To understand language, you not only have to have the ability to use it, but more importantly you have to actively *produce* and indeed *transform* it. Reading, writing, listening, speaking and viewing are all practices which entail use, production and transformation. Context enables meaning-making to take place. In a schooling context, essay-writing enables students to understand and derive success in a particular form of school literacy, expository writing. In a home context, creating an interface for a website is a particular form of literacy which enables a child to understand and derive success in their own world. In Chapter 3 the home and school domains are considered side by side and brought together.

WHY DOES IDENTITY BREATHE LIFE INTO LITERACY?

Or, why should we consider identity as at the heart of language teaching? We have as many different language learners in our classrooms as there are personalities within our classroom space. Our students bring so many rich language experiences and differing levels of understanding of schooled language that we need to build our teaching around difference as opposed to a standardized, one-size-fits-all approach that we have adopted over the past decade. To take account of the local, we are also saying that we need to take account of identities within different spaces. However, to achieve a third space in our language teaching means a space that speaks to the needs of different types of language learners.

In Chapters 5 and 6, we supply a roadmap for implementing a curriculum for multiple identities, multimodality and multiliteracies. However, we acknowledge that this is not going to happen overnight. So, we bring vignettes from different spaces to illustrate how other teachers have adapted these different frameworks for their own students. Within local contexts, teachers respond to their students' identities. It is a more equitable form of teaching if student identities are brought to the fore.

WHY CELEBRATE THE MICRO?

Recently, while observing classrooms in Sheffield and Toronto, we noticed how many teachers are already mediating the literacy curriculum. Their students engage with web spaces, they construct cultural artefacts from bits of stuff from home, they tell stories which draw on a wealth of cultural experience. When working and observing in classrooms, we have been aware of how teachers' practices are sometimes unrecorded, and need lifting from the micro contexts into the macro contexts of government curricula. We have written this book to celebrate the local practices of teachers as well as to bring new theories into the world of literacy. However, by focusing on the micro and the local, we can infuse the macro and the global with the same expressive power. When children's texts cross sites, and move from home to school, teachers are facilitating learning spaces that can then be opened up further. They are making spaces for learning. This book explores what happens when local practices are recognized in new contexts, and educational contexts offer literacy practices recognition. By supporting literacy across a range of contexts, the field of literacy is enriched and strengthened.

WHY READ THIS BOOK?

We hope that this book will be used to generate debate and offer inspiration to teachers. We have used vignettes to situate our accounts of practice. We also offer activities, to stimulate thinking. In addition, theoretical ideas are placed within theory boxes, to allow access to key concepts in the New Literacy Studies. We aim to bring theory closer to practice, and to link up different threads in doing so. A glossary of key terms (emboldened at first occurence in text) will also help you navigate the ideas in this book. We bring to a wider audience the new debates within literacy, drawing on a number of different fields. However, we hope above all that this book will be practical as well as inspirational.

CHAPTER 1

The New Literacy Studies and Teaching Literacy: Where We Were and Where We Are Going

Vignette: *Designing dual-language books*

A child is making a book. However, the child is not using paper and pens. She is sitting at a computer screen. She is not even writing. She is looking at a number of different images on screen. These images are drawings she has done at home. They are images she has previously drawn. They are being selected to create a dual-language text, in the child's home language, Chinese, and in the language used at school, English. The child selects the drawing she thinks goes together with the words, which she has already composed also in Chinese, and places them side by side using a mouse. She is making a book, using drawings she did at home and scanned into the computer, and words constructed together with her mother, from stories she has heard, at home. The words were then written with the help of her teacher. The finished book has hand-drawn pictures, writing in English, and writing in Chinese, side by side. The book will be used by other children learning to read in Chinese and English, and their parents, at school and in homes. (Vignette courtesy of J. Cummins, keynote talk, British Association for Applied Linguistics, 2003.)

KEY THEMES IN THE CHAPTER

- *Literacy as a social practice*
- *Literacy as an event and a set of practices*
- *Literacy as a global and local practice*

INTRODUCTION

Imagine that you are teaching students who have been identified as 'under-achieving in literacy'. These are young teenagers who come from a number of different backgrounds. In your classroom you are teaching students from a number of war-torn countries. With time, you appreciate that your students all love music. In their out-of-school lives they listen to rap music, and enjoy surfing the Web at the local Internet café. Instead of shutting out this experience, you bring it in. You encourage students to look at words in rap songs, and discuss poetry, metaphor and assonance, using words from Eminem. These students begin to engage with literacy, to write poetry and to tell their life stories. You have drawn on their out-of-school literacies to engage them in the classroom.

The vignette that begins the chapter comes from a Canadian classroom. It depicts the multiplicity of literacy practices involved in making a book for children to use in classrooms. It begins a journey into key themes introduced in this chapter and at the heart of the book.

The view of literacy as a **social practice**, is one of the key themes of this chapter. In the vignette, the child drew on the social practice of story-telling to compose a story. An aim of this book is to open your eyes to the multiplicity of literacy practices that exist around us, and to see how this understanding can be applied to classrooms where students engage with literacy practices. In this chapter, the concepts behind the idea of literacy as a social practice will be explained, and you will be introduced to key ideas, including the idea of **literacy events** and **literacy practices**.

The moment of composing a **text** can be described as a *literacy event*, an event in which literacy forms a part. Part of the composing process draws on a child's experience of literacy practices, particularly the practice of reading books and the practice of writing and composing in classrooms. This view of literacy can be contrasted with a view of literacy as a set of skills. In this book, we argue that it is possible to combine an understanding of literacy as a set of skills *with* an understanding of how we use literacy in everyday life. In fact, we argue that if we bring these understandings together, it helps. What is more, we consider how the idea of literacy as a social practice encourages our students' writing and reading development in classroom settings.

When our students write, they draw on cultural experiences they have had in their lives. They may come from different parts of the globe, and then sit within an urbanized space. They may live in a remote rural community, on an island, but be connected to the world through the Internet. If literacy is understood as a *global and social practice*, this helps us understand why children need to communicate not only across different cultures, but also in relation to changing global communication.

This thought can be understood in relation to the opening vignette. When the child at the beginning of this chapter drew on her own script in Chinese, she was drawing on her identity as a child who speaks Chinese, and was locating her global identity alongside the local identity within the classroom. The Internet and email make communicating different – and even closer than ever before. This field has been identified with **literacy** and **globalization**. In Chapter 4, the link between global literacy practices and local literacy practices will be explored, especially with regard to students in classrooms. For example, how do your students view the Internet? As a way of finding out about science projects? As a place to meet and chat with others? Or as a literacy practice?

The concept of literacy as a social practice helps us to see literacy as connected to other things. For example, when you go to a bank and fill in a form, you are engaging with literacy as a social practice. This social practice links up with other social practices, for example, banking practices. When we type on screen we are situated within a specific time and place as we type, but as we open up our email the world comes rushing in. The global practices from the World Wide Web infuse our local spaces.

When our students write and read, they infuse these practices into their identities. Literacy learners bring their identities into the making of meaning, and as they learn to read, or put marks on a page, their cultural experience goes before them, and their marks are inscribed with that experience. This book connects to new ideas about the relationship between literacy and **identity** and how this works in classrooms. You will also consider what this perspective does to aid classroom practice. Identities are complex, made up of hybrid and multiple experiences. Identities shape our literacy practices. These identity-infused literacy practices are then taken up in school and encounter different literacy practices. How can we ensure that our students' literacy practices in classrooms account for their identities out of school?

For example, thinking back to the child in the vignette at the beginning of the chapter, how was her identity upheld by her work in making stories? If we consider the child's cultural identity in relation to her literacy practices, she is experiencing a positive link between the child as a person reading stories in the home and her identity in school. The child's identity as a

Chinese speaker is recognized alongside the child's identity as an English speaker, by constructing the text as a dual-language book. Through use of the dual language, and by giving the child space to draw her own illustrations, her home identity and her schooled identity are brought closer together through the school project of making a book.

These themes might prompt you to reflect on the following *key questions*:

- How do your students' home/out-of-the-classroom literacy practices contrast with your students' literacy practices in a learning situation?

- What are the links between literacy practices and the learning of literacy skills?

- How do the tools used to support literacy learning in an educational setting confirm or not confirm your students' sense of identity?

These questions are the focus of this chapter. The following section explains where you can find the theory behind these ideas, and how you can use these theories to understand literacy practices.

THE NEW LITERACY STUDIES: AN OVERVIEW

This section introduces you to some of the key thinkers in this field, which has been identified as the **New Literacy Studies**. The term has been used in relation to a number of scholars who looked at literacy in everyday life (Street, 1984; Gee, 1996; Barton and Hamilton, 1998). They drew on research on communication and on anthropology to look at the role of literacy in people's lives. There are many people associated with the New Literacy Studies. In this section, we offer an overview to a wide field.

Research from the New Literacy Studies examines literacy practices, and literacy events, and many researchers have used it's perspective to look at what people do with literacy. Because of studies looking at how people used literacy in everyday life, the concept of literacy began to be rethought. Previously, literacy was something associated with books and writing, and perceived as a set of skills, which were taught in schools. More recently, literacy has been recognized as a social practice, something that people do in everyday life, in their homes, at work and at school. For example, in an ethnographic study in Lancaster, researchers watched people write notes at allotment meetings and observed people read to their children, and write diaries, letters and poems at home for pleasure (Barton and Hamilton, 1998).

As an example, consider the banking description given earlier. If this is described in terms of literacy practices, it could look like this:

Literacy event	Literacy practice	Social practice
Signing the bank cheque	Filling the cheque in – form filling	Banking

A literacy event is the observed event, often most easily spotted in the class-room. When your students write and read, they are engaged in a set of literacy events. These events are often regular, and relate to the practices of reading and writing. A student will read a book as part of the literacy practice of book reading in the classroom.

In considering the New Literacy Studies, the field has been shaped by people. They have gone out and thought and watched people, and then have written up their ideas. You will find below some of the most impor-tant ideas that contribute to this field, along with people who have contributed to them.

Sylvia Scribner and Michael Cole: Literacy practices in different domains

Sylvia Scribner and Michael Cole were psychologists who studied the Vai people of West Africa, in Liberia. They wanted to understand the relation-ship between local cultural contexts and the learning of literacy. Unusually, the people they studied, the Vai, had invented an original writ-ing system, which was learned outside of school. The school language was English, and the schools for the Qu'ran used Arabic. Scribner and Cole studied the different language practices within the different settings. They found that specific types of literacy practices affected how people learned things. Scribner and Cole taught us that there is not just one literacy, but many forms of literacy, all linked to different domains of practice. The published study, *The Psychology of Literacy*, became a key text in the history of the New Literacy Studies, in that for the first time literacy practices were described in different **domains** of practice (Scribner and Cole, 1981).

Mapping literacy practices across sites is a fruitful task. Spaces provide dif-ferent kinds of opportunities for literacy practices. Spaces offer people multiple identities. These different identities infuse their literacy practices.

A study of literacy and space offers the opportunity to think about what people do with literacy in different spaces.

The word 'domain' refers to a particular **space**, or world where literacy is practised (for example, the Church, the school, the home). Researchers have identified a number of literacy practices within different domains. Multiple identities come to the fore in specific domains. You may express yourself differently in a formal letter written at work, than in an email written to a friend at home.

ACTIVITY

Writing and identity

Think about some writing you have done which you feel strongly about. This could be a letter to a Member of Parliament, a piece of poetry, even an assignment you were very fond of. How did that affect the way you wrote and how you wrote? How does your **identity-in-practice** shape your writing style?

A domain can be identified with a way of being, and in many cases, as a set of cultural beliefs, or a world view. Sometimes it is site-specific, such as a school, with buildings, but sometimes literacy practices from one domain, such as school, cross to another, such as home. Homework is an example of a literacy practice which is from the school domain, but is carried out in the home site.

Brian V. Street: Ideological or autonomous literacies

Brian Street, working as a social anthropologist in Iran, also described literacy practices in different domains. He conducted fieldwork in the village where he lived which focused on literacy practices in different domains. These included what he termed:

maktab literacy, or literacy associated with Islam and taught in the local Qur'anic schools;

commercial literacy, or the reading and writing used for the management of fruit sales in the local village;

school literacy, associated with the state schools more recently built in the villages and located in the urban areas as well.

This description of literacy enabled Street to identify how particular views of literacy were linked to particular ways of thinking (Street, 1984). From this, Street developed the concepts of *ideological* and *autonomous* literacy. He argued that literacy has been viewed, in particular by government agencies, as a separate, thing-like object which people should acquire, as a set of decontextualized skills. This view of literacy sees literacy as a technical skill. Writing, in particular, can be viewed as an autonomous skill, which can be related to individual cognitive processes. Street identified this view with a certain governmental trend to think of literacy as a set of skills which can be acquired. However, this view of literacy did not take into consideration how people used literacy. Instead, he argued, the term **ideological** could be used to describe the way in which literacy is grounded in how it is used, and how it relates to power structures within society (Street, 1993).

Street therefore challenged us not to see literacy as a neutral skill, but as a *socially situated practice*. This was a key insight within the field known as the New Literacy Studies.

REFLECTION

When can literacy be regarded as shaped by cultural and ideological forces?

And when is it written down as a set of skills?

Consider ways in which literacy is described where you work, and how it is regarded.

How does it change when you consider it as a reflection of social and **cultural practice**?

Shirley Brice Heath: Literacy events and literacy practices

In the 1970s, in the rural Carolinas, another area of literacy was being researched. Shirley Brice Heath, and her team of researchers, were considering how different communities used and interacted around literacy. *Ways with Words* described the different language and literacy practices of two communities in the rural Carolinas, USA. In the book, Heath contrasted a black community, Trackton, with a white working-class community,

Roadville. She paid close attention to the way parents in these two communities spoke to their children, raised them, how they decorated their homes and how the children interacted with their parents. Then she looked at what happened when they went to school. In the case of both Trackton and Roadville children, there was a disjuncture between their home literacy practices and their school literacy practices. This was in contrast to the children from the town. Heath called the town community Maintown. The children in Maintown were teacher's children, who had been raised and talked to in a way which echoed the norms of 'school' literacy. In order to understand how different ways of interacting contributed to different outcomes in literacy, Heath focused her study around the concept of *literacy events* which she defined, as, 'any action sequence, involving one or more persons, in which the production and/or comprehension of print plays a role' (Heath, 1983: 386). This concept enabled Heath to understand in a contrastive way the different events and practices around literacy, by isolating specific instances. Heath also looked at communicative utterances and contrasted them across the communities.

For example, Heath describes how a $2^1/_2$-year-old named Lem made an oral response to his experience of hearing a distant bell ring, which meshed with his experience of Church going,

> *Way Far*
> *Now*
> *It a Church bell*
> *Ringin'*
> *Dey singin'*
> *Ringin'*
> *You hear it?*
> *I hear it*
> *Far*
> *Now*
>
> (Heath, 1983: 170)

Heath isolated this piece of oral talk, almost a poem, as one which was deeply embedded within the community's oral traditions, but did not have a corresponding link to classrooms.

Her work led many researchers to look more closely at literacy practices in homes and communities. In this chapter, we ask you to consider what Heath's study could tell you in your teaching. Could it be used to consider how the literacy practices of school contrast with those of your students' out-of-school literacy practices?

THE ETHNOGRAPHY OF COMMUNICATION

Heath's work came from a tradition called the *ethnography of communication*, which understood how it was possible to understand different communicative events in different settings. By combining **ethnography** – as a way of studying different contexts and grounded in a particular methodological frame – with communication – the study of how people communicate – the ethnography of communication conceived of a richer understanding of literacy and language skills. This has relevance to institutional settings such as schools. Dell Hymes, in particular, was able to describe why African-American children sometimes were not succeeding in schools. African-American forms of speech and narrative structures often differed from those of their white counterparts (Hymes, 1996). This led to African-American children's **narratives** not being recognized in classroom settings. Hymes argued that we do not appreciate narrative as a form of knowledge. Indeed, we under-appreciate the ways in which speech patterns are recognized in different contexts. A key concept to describe language in use is *discourse*. Hymes's work on the ethnography of communication can be linked to work by James Paul Gee on discourse and language patterns of different linguistic communities.

Gee's work on discourse

James Paul Gee has worked both within the New Literacy Studies and within the ethnography of communication. Gee developed theories of language which viewed language as socially situated. Gee argued that when we try to understand a person's language-in-use, or discourse, we not only pay attention to the accent, intonation and speech style of that person, among other things, but also we pay attention to that person's style of clothing, gestures, and bodily movements. He calls language-in-use **discourse**. When he talks about language plus other stuff he uses the term **Discourse** (Gee, 1999).

DISCOURSE, IDENTITY AND LITERACY

Gee's concept of discourse can be used with reference to a classroom. Students bring the different Discourses they are involved with into the classroom setting, for example, teenagers may locate their **discursive identity** in clothes, their way of speaking, their artefacts, such as mobile phones, and so on. Language is rarely the only way we display our identity. As Gee said,

> To 'pull off' being an 'X' doing 'Y' (eg a Los Angeles Latino street-gang member warning another gang member off his territory, or a laboratory physicist warning another laboratory physicist off her research territory) it is not enough to get just the words 'right', though that is crucial. It is necessary, as well, to get one's body, clothes, gestures, actions, interactions, ways with things, symbols, tools, technologies (be they guns or graphs), and values, attitudes, beliefs, and emotions 'right' as well, and all at the 'right' places and times.
> When 'little d' discourse (language-in-use) is melded integrally with non-language 'stuff' to enact specific identities and activities, then, I say that 'big D' Discourses are involved. We are all members of a many, a great many, different Discourses, Discourses which often influence each other in positive and negative ways, and which sometimes breed with each other to create new hybrids. (Gee, 1999: 7)

This can be understood like this:

discourse	Language-in-use
Discourse	Language-in-use plus other stuff

Literacy and learning practices are embedded in various Discourses, or ways of knowing, doing, talking, reading and writing, which are constructed and reproduced in social and cultural practice and interaction. Literacy practices are inextricably linked to oral language and how it is used. Gee's work focused on how we interact with one another, and on how the words we use are important as well as the accent, gestures, tone and body.

Discourses can represent the ways we signal our identities. Our ways of dressing, speaking and acting all signal our membership of different identities in practice. Gee considered that people can occupy different, or multiple identities, in relation to the different discourse communities we occupy. We might be a parent in one context, a teacher in another, a member of a band in another. We can move between these identities as we go about our life. Gee, like other scholars spotlighted in the chapter, located literacy within society. He saw how literacy was shaped by how we use it. He wanted us to understand literacy as socially situated in order to foreground why school versions of literacy help some students, while hindering others. In doing so, he asked that we look at literacy and power.

David Barton and Mary Hamilton: Local literacies

The work of Barton, Hamilton, Ivanic and others at Lancaster, has focused on how literacy practices mesh with everyday lives. In a series of studies, the socially situated nature of literacy was explored and documented. Literacy practices could be observed in communities by analysing notes taken at an allotment meeting, through hearing about the reading of a bedtime story to a child or through documenting the writing of letters from prison. All these different literacy practices were associated with different domains of life, such as home, community and classroom.

Barton and Hamilton examined the role of literacy practices and literacy events in people's lives in Lancaster. Their book, *Local Literacies*, explored the complex web of literacy practices that people engaged with. Barton and Hamilton came up with the idea of **ruling passions** to explain how people's interests often dictated their literacy practices. People's ruling passions varied: pop stars, gardening, hobbies and a host of other interests guided people's literacy practices. These ruling passions enabled researchers to get at why literacy mattered to people, and what they used literacy for (Barton and Hamilton, 1998).

This work enables us to look at how we use literacy in everyday life, and where we use different literacies. By associating **multiple literacies** with different domains, we can trace across a number of spaces the multiple ways literacy is used.

ACTIVITY

The domains of literacy

Divide your world into domains (that is, places where literacy is carried out, for example, home, workplace, community, and so on). Within each domain, write a brief account of the literacy events you engage in. Note which are different, and which are the same. Make a list of social practices that underpin the identified event. Making a shopping list, for example, is linked to the **social practice** of shopping.

WHY DOES LITERACY NEED THE NEW LITERACY STUDIES?

This is a space to reflect on what these ideas can offer the practitioner. You have read above how there are particular literacy practices associated with different domains, that is, spaces in life. School is just one space where literacy practices occur. However, there are other places where literacy practices have developed. Does it help to understand how students use literacy in different domains of their lives? Are these forms of literacy different? Do children, when they go onto the Internet and click at their favourite pictures, still use literacy?

If you consider your students, one of the key aspects of your work is to support them in their literacy practices. You might notice a student has an interest in a particular country, such as Turkey, based on his cultural identity. You could then ask the student to draw a map of Turkey. The student could then work on telling some stories from Turkey, or describing some home practices using Turkish as a medium for the story. These practices could be playing console games, or watching Turkish television.

The child in the vignette at the start of the chapter was drawing on a different domain of literacy, the home domain, in order to make her book. More importantly, she was drawing on a panoply of 'skills': decoding and encoding print; viewing and representing; visual communication; multiple literacies (Chinese and English); multimodal meaning-making (choosing a font and colour scheme); and interpersonal relationships and home–school ties (her Mum and her teacher). She was also drawing on a number of literacy events embedded in practices, including the practice of her mother telling her a story in her home language, Chinese. The vignette also illustrates the importance of the connection of domains of home and school for learners to succeed, and for that as a way of overcoming possible distances between home and school.

In this book, we argue that the New Literacy Studies opens up our frame of reference about literacy. It makes us aware of our learners in relation to their identities. Literacy learners produce texts – bits of writing and other expressions of meaning, like drawing and talking. They become makers of texts and, as such, they infuse their texts with their sense of identity. They also are receivers of texts, which are embedded with all the everyday life things that happen to people. These include shopping and cooking and watching television as well as a myriad other practices, all interwoven into the act of being literate.

It is possible to observe how in ordinary life people draw on different literacy practices at different times in their lives: filling in forms, writing a letter and writing for leisure or work purposes. Children in families draw and write as part of their communicative practices. If you share your home with a child, you will recognize how children may make marks, draw and write as part of a spectrum of communication, which includes literacy. Some of these bits of paper you will keep, and others you will throw away. In a recent study of three London homes 'mess' was connected up with children's communicative practices: drawings and bits of writing on paper were often seen as 'stuff' to be tidied up and thrown away (Pahl, 2002).

So what does the New Literacy Studies offer the classroom? The New Literacy Studies offers both a new way of looking at students, as involved in literacy in a number of different domains, and a way of seeing literacy in the classroom, as part of everyday life, meshed in with everything else. It makes the classroom both local and global.

Bits of literacy can be discovered in different spaces. Literacy is present on the street, and students can use their experience of street life and community spaces to document those in-between spaces. Many children attend after-school clubs where they play games and draw, attending to different parts of their literacy practices.

The classroom is simply one domain where literacy occurs, but not the only one. Your classroom can reflect **local** domains: shopping, the school journey, the local area; or **global**: the Internet, console games, popular films, raps and stories. Children's popular **culture** offers a range of ideas to link in with your students' literacy experiences out of school. In the next section, we hone in on some of the concepts from the New Literacy Studies which might be particularly helpful.

Using New Literacy Studies in classrooms

1   Jot down or have your students jot down all types of reading, writing, viewing, and representing they do at home. Provide examples from your own life. Have them get into pairs to compare and contrast their list.

2   Make posters to advertise websites, films, books, console games, or any print media.

3   Identify parts of speech used in such popular media as comic books, game card rule books, or websites. Talk about the types of verbs, nouns, adjectives and pronouns used.

> **4** Ask students to find ways of expressing shock or terror or humour or joy or other types of emotion in multiple writing contexts, such as comics, letters to friends, emails or texting.
>
> **5** Ask students to find different versions — across cultures — of a classic story like Cinderella.
>
> **6** Talk about the format and layout of different genres of text — print and electronic.

REFLECTION ON LITERACY EVENTS AND LITERACY PRACTICES

In this section, we reflect a little more on why the concept of literacy events and literacy practices helps us teach our students. For example, it gives you an opportunity to describe a moment when your student reads a piece of text in class as a *literacy event*. Literacy events can be found in formal and informal settings, when a student writes an essay, or when your child writes a birthday card. By putting a name on the practice, the event can be analysed.

The link between events and practices is one that is worth reflecting on. While you may connect a literacy event to a classroom setting, a literacy practice is often connected to out-of-classroom settings and can be observed as a regular, iterative event. Iterative implies that something happens over and over again. Many practices have this quality: in a mosque, the same prayers are heard, in a church, the Liturgy is the same every week. Many families have things they do on a regular basis, and literacy practices fit into this: thank-you letters to relatives, or birthday cards to friends. We can hold a literacy practice in our heads from one day to the next. The practice of filling in a form can be drawn upon when filling in a new form.

> ## Vignette: Liturgy class as a literacy practice
>
> *For some time, Rita Gravina, a secondary teacher in Toronto, prepared children for their first Communion by offering liturgy classes at a neighbouring Roman Catholic church. By participating in a number of activities and events on a weekly basis, children became full members of the Catholic Church. During each session, children listened to messages offered by Rita and the parish priest. What Rita noted over the course of these sessions were several literacy events that inducted children into a Christian identity. For example, a literacy event that took place is children were given a variety of physical objects used in a Catholic mass. Some of these included: 'the*

Bible containing God's words, the chalice containing wine which is representative of Jesus' blood and the chalice containing the Eucharist which is to be representative of Jesus' body which he sacrificed on the cross' (Reflection written by Rita Gravina). Each child was asked to pick up these objects and to think about what these were and how they were used. Student responses varied, which reflected their own experiences and cultural and family backgrounds. The literacy event showed that each child could bring their experience and their identity to create meaning in an outside space.

The following activity helps you think about domains of literacy. It also encourages you to consider how literacy is seen in that domain. It draws on the words **autonomous** and **ideological** from Street's work.

He saw the words as meaning:

Autonomous	Ideological
Literacy as a separate 'thing', as a set of skills	Literacy as connected with cultural and social practices in the world

The following activity connects up your thinking on literacy events and practices, with the idea of autonomous and ideological models of literacy.

ACTIVITY

Literacy events and literacy practices

Go back to your list of literacy events and the practices which situated them. Which of these are linked to autonomous models of literacy, and which are linked to ideological models?

For example, a lot of workplace literacy practices, such as form-filling, are linked to an ideological model of literacy. Make a list of the domains which include the more autonomous literacy practices.

If you are currently working with a model of curriculum, reflect on which domain this model relates to, the ideological model or the autonomous model of literacy.

LITERACY AND POWER

In their introduction to *Situated Literacies* Barton, Hamilton and Ivanic argue that, 'Literacy practices are patterned by social institutions and power relations, and some literacies are more dominant, visible and influential than others'. (Barton, Hamilton and Ivanic, 2000: 12)

It is important to recognize how different literacy practices shape the way we interact with literacy. Literacy is not value-free. Some discourses are more dominant than others. In some cases, we have to fit in with dominant models of literacy such as curricula. In this book, we do not refer to specific curricula, such as the National Literacy Strategy in the UK, but prefer to work with this idea of literacy as a social practice. The National Literacy Strategy is a literacy practice, imbued with the **traces** of its making. *It is not neutral.*

Individuals use literacy, as do groups. It can act as a resource for people, and a way of becoming empowered (Barton and Hamilton, 2000: 13). In this book, we also see it as a way of expressing identities, either as a group or individually, in particular domains. Our histories of literacy trace our own practices. Thinking back to when we were children, we can trace how we developed in the different ways we used literacy. We are shaped by the way we use literacy. Our unofficial hidden literacy practices are as important as the public, institutional ones we participate in. Rather than focus on one sort of literacy, here we focus on the multiple ways we use literacy, but recognizing that some are more heard and more visible than others. This book acknowledges that meaning can be made from a variety of modes, and some students may learn better using a multiplicity of modes. This chapter makes a point that you can look more closely at your students' communicative practices in order to find clues as to how to develop your teaching in response to them. This brings more equity into the classroom.

CONCLUSION

Literacy is bound up with our identity and our practices. The shaping of our literacy practices takes place in a number of different domains, for example, home, school and workplace. Taking on an approach that looks at literacy as a social practice involves a number of key thoughts. It involves acknowledging that school is only one setting where literacy takes place. It recognizes that the resources used to teach in classrooms might be different from the resources used by students in their homes. To conclude this section, who we are and who we are allowed to be is shaped in part by the way we use literacy.

The literacy practices we use, however, may include multiple forms of representation. Like the child at the beginning of the chapter, we may use the computer and digitally manipulate material to create cards, messages and stories. When we engage with literacy we are also engaging with the visual. We discuss this at greater length in Chapter 2. Our understandings of what it means to be literate need to include other forms of symbol-making. This could include icons used on the screen, **symbols** and **signs** associated with the cultural spaces we occupy, drawings and photographs, which connect to oral and literacy practices. We will now explore this new communicational landscape and consider what this means for literacy.

CHAPTER 2

Multimodal Literacies: New Ways of Reading and Writing

Vignette: Multimodal literacies and game cards

In Angie Comia's year 3 classroom in a suburban school, she frequently observes boys trading Pokémon, Digimon and Yu-Gi-Oh cards. As she puts it, 'the boys would immerse themselves in an entirely different language in the Pokémon, Digimon, or Yu-Gi-Oh worlds'. They knew hundreds of different characters that existed and they knew the functions and idiosyncrasies of each one. Some of the boys interacted with these texts in different ways using verbal skills, role-play, bodily movement and reasoning skills. They accepted the rules and the consequences that went with trading the cards. They watched these characters on television and interacted digitally with characters and games via the Internet and websites. In short, they were ensconced in the culture of these texts and the texts presided over their social worlds.

Angela decided to research characterization and storyline in the cards, games and other forms of texts. She found all sorts of evidence of literacy in instructions printed on the back of cards and rule books with elaborate information about each card. For the final writing assignment of the year, Angela asked her class to publish a storybook. She encouraged the group of boys to write about what they love to read. Each one produced books on Pokémon, Digimon, or Yu-Gi-Oh that had covers, illustrations, rule books and instructions. What is more, each boy became passionate about the process, about the practices used to publish the texts and about the texts themselves.

INTRODUCTION

Imagine you have two books in front of you. One is an older, reading-scheme reader; the other is *Jazzy in the Jungle* by Lucy Cousins. As you leaf through them you note that while one uses pictures to support the writing and has a standard storyline, the other book has some written text, but most of the story relies on lifting flaps to understand the storyline. The more traditional book has to be read in sequence, whereas the contemporary text can be read from back to front and still be understood. In one, the written explains the visual, in the other the visual explains the written. Where one book has naturalistic pictures in pastel, the other has stylized pictures in bold reds, blues, greens and gold. One book you can hold in your hand and one can be read by a couple of students on their laps. One is predictable; the other is full of surprises. Turning the pages, children are far more likely to reach for the visual, tactile book than they are the Dick and Jane reader. What is it that makes reading and writing different today than it was a decade or two ago? The answer lies in multimodality; in a concept of communication that subsumes the written, the visual, the gestural and the tactile into one entity – a multimodal text.

WHAT IS OUR WORLD TODAY?

The students we teach are already in contact with the world of new technology, with the computer screen, the console game, the television screen and the visual world of advertising. They live in local spaces, infused with global advertising and a plethora of images. In this chapter we ask the following key questions:

- ■ How do we define texts?

- ■ How do we teach the texts our learners read?

- ■ How do we read these new texts?

- ■ How do you help learners navigate these texts?

It helps to consider the types of texts our students use, which are releva to literacy teaching:

- Storybooks
- Non-fiction books (for example, Dorling Kindersley books)
- Fables
- Pop-up and lift-the-flap books
- Web pages and weblogs
- Advertisements
- Poetry

- Songs
- Artwork
- Texting
- Cartoons
- Movies
- Animated films
- Videogames
- Logos and graphics

The chapter explores new ways of seeing texts. In this chapter, we draw on Gee's concept of Discourses. These are ways of speaking, behaving and acting in culturally specific ways as described in Chapter 1. Texts are seen as carrying different Discourses, as made up of visuals, sound, movement and gesture. Texts can be seen as **artefacts** that trace back to people and places. Take a book you are currently reading and consider that this book contains a history of the writing and the publishing within it. It may contain echoes of other texts, other communicative artefacts. It will feel a certain way, have a certain typeface and cover. The decisions about what it looks like will have been made by people along the way. In Rowsell's work, she traces back the publishing of reading books for children, exposing them as **traces** of social practice (Rowsell, 2000).

TEXTS AS ARTEFACTS

Literacy educators need to redefine the way we see and interact with texts. We need to see **texts as artefacts**, that is, as objects with a history and as a material presence. In this chapter we use the word *multimodal* to describe the way we communicate, using a number of different modes to make meaning. A mode could be visual, linguistic, aural or tactile.

Multimodality can be seen in every text and has shifted how children engage with literacy. Students no longer simply decode, skim and scan, but they move across and among texts, design texts, create mark-up code, render images, and so on. Where students formerly understood the layout of pages in a book, today students read, design, surf and write on-screen. Students as readers of modern texts are accustomed to reading for information as it is supplied versus completing a text and moving on. They work from one byte of information to the next and can move between and among screens to gather information and bring it together in an essay they are writing for school. Information now is immediate and not a trip to the library to leaf through books for what we need. These skills imply new sets of practices students have to master as readers and writers. In this chapter we will discuss theorists, feature vignettes, supply strategies, and provide activities for working within a multimodal approach to language.

WHERE IS MULTIMODALITY?

We see multimodality in popular media in such animated texts as *Bob the Builder* and *Jimmy Neutron*, which have been translated into different languages around the world. Multimodal texts such as these have 'universal' appeal and purpose, but meaning is made from them in local contexts. Although modern texts move across sites (for example, from school to home) and invite new sets of practices with different users, the content, design and multimodality remain the same. As educators, we should not only understand and use these modern texts, but also come to understand their place within our classrooms.

Vignette: Sam's multimodal meaning-making at home

Sam, a 6-year-old boy, loved Pokémon and spent a great deal of time at home playing with his Pokémon cards. He had hundreds of them. However, he didn't just play with them. Sam liked to cut them out, and re-fashion them, using collage to develop cards of his own. Figure 2.1 shows Sam's 'Trainer' card, a new card made up of bits and pieces cut out of magazines, and stuck together. The card has been made up of a number of different cut-out bits and has acquired a life of its own. The card was a 'trainer card' for Sam, who described the process: 'I got Japanese Pokémons from a magazine cut out the picture and then I just got my Porygon card 'cos I got 2 of them. It has the same moves I cut out trainer and stick on its name. I cutted the picture out and stuck it on there.'

Sam referred back to this process to me as we played in his bedroom. 'That was a Porygon card but he's made of collage but he's stuck together and I made him because of that.'

Here, the 'cutting out' involved a transformation – from one kind of Pokémon card to another – a 'trainer' which can be used in the Pokémon card game to develop the characteristics of individual cards. Sam effected his transformation with the representational resources available to him. The

---

▶

materiality of this card, and this emphasis on the new name, using new bits of Pokémon card, is how Sam signalled the difference between the 'real' Pokémon card and his new one. Here, the multimodal aspect of the card, its form and shape, signalled the meaning (Pahl, 2003).

Figure 2.1 Sam's trainer card

WHAT DO WE DO WITH TEXTS?

When we write an essay, or set up a classroom task, we think about its use, its intended practice. By *intended practices* we are referring to how the producer or producers *intend* the text to be used (at home, at school, in groups, in pairs, reading on your own in a chair, and so on). Texts look the way they do because a person or group of people designed them that way: for a particular audience, to use them at a particular time, in a particular space. The resulting text is therefore filled with identity, differing points of view and different intended ways of using it.

THE WAY WE FEEL ABOUT TEXTS

When we create a text, we do so in relation to our interest, how we feel, how we construct it in our minds. What underpins this chapter is a belief that texts of all kinds are produced based on the *interest* of the producer.

For example, when a child draws a circle with lines in the centre, it can depict a multitude of things. Figure 2.2, drawn by a 2-year-old child, depicts important people in a child's world – her Dad, her Mum, her caregiver, her cousin, and so on.

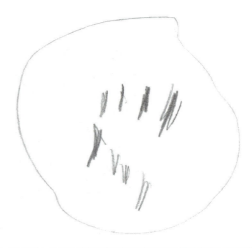

Figure 2.2 Community circle

Textbooks we use in class look and sound the way they do because publishers intended them to look and to sound that way with a particular audience in mind. Equally, advertisements on the Internet or television have an intended audience with intended outcomes. Newspapers are designed and written so that a specific readership with a particular lifestyle will read them, perhaps even in a certain place at a certain time. Texts of all kinds arise out of the interest at a given moment and the design and content reflect these decisions.

THE MOTIVATED SIGN

Texts therefore carry the motivations of the producer (child, songwriter, publisher, poet, and so on) or, as Kress expresses it, texts are *motivated signs* (Kress, 1997). How we choose to make a text of any kind bespeaks our identity. Kress speaks of 'best ways' of representing meanings. In some circumstances, meanings are best expressed through words and pictures, whereas in others, movement or three dimensions might be preferable. Children's artefacts carry with them the choices they made during the process – why they opted for red sweeps of colour with a bit of green (Figure 2.3) vs purple sweeps of colour with a bit of green.

Figure 2.3 Red sweeps with a bit of green

CREATIVITY IN TEXTUAL FORMS

Children are guided far more by what Kress refers to as *synaesthetic activities*. They are not as influenced as adults are by the predominance of written text, and tend to be guided more by other modes such as the visual, kinaesthetic, three-dimensional and gestural modes. They draw on these different modes freely when making meaning, and may not see one as more salient than another. Instead, children may choose the most appropriate mode for their meaning-making activities.

The notion of **synaesthesia** is much like our notion of creativity and creative expression. Creativity and synaesthesia rely on all of the senses when we make meaning. The artefacts we make reflect synaesthetic activity being composed of sound, of materials, of words, and so on. In early years settings, creativity is in full bloom in the types of texts used and the materials used to create them. Take Madeleine's two drawings (Figure 2.2 and 2.3), she decided what mode worked best, based on her synaesthetic instincts (for example, lines in a circle represent people to whom she is close). As our schooling progresses into the junior and intermediate years, creative expression or synaesthetic activity changes, and there is far more of a focus on the written *and* skills acquisition. Once children enter school, there is a privileging of the written over other modes. Schooled literacy focuses on written language above and beyond other, alternative, modes.

ACTIVITY

Tracing interest in texts

Find or think of a text of any kind — an essay for a course, a work of art, a picture book — and describe the process of making the text.

> What other choices did you or the author have in its production?
>
> What senses does the text draw upon?
>
> Why do you think the author is drawing upon these particular senses?
>
> How could you have designed the text differently?
>
> Can you locate the author in the work?
>
> Can you locate the context in which it was made?
>
> Does the language speak to a particular community?

MATERIALITY OF TEXTS

In *Before Writing*, Kress asks an important question which is salient today given all of the shifts in reading and writing practices: what kind of reader do we want to produce and for what and whose ends (Kress, 1997)? The question is polemical in that we all must read and write in certain ways to work and fulfil daily lives. However, at the same time, the question is central when educating school children. This question takes account of the different texts the children we teach encounter in their daily lives.

Our understanding of texts, on content, structural and visual levels, guides the way we read and produce future texts. We learn about writing from our past experiences as a reader and a writer. These past experiences guide our writing. When we write a piece of fiction, we draw on our experience of stories. We cobble together our conception of writing within a genre by reading other texts within that genre.

Similarly, children who watch animated texts like *Shrek* or *Dora the Explorer* incorporate phrases from these texts into their own speech. Children often acquire idioms and turns of phrases in their viewing of videos or DVDs.

Gee argues that children actually think and use language in different, more complex ways by using videogames.

Gee on meaning-making and videogames

James Paul Gee, claims that in the 'space' or use of videogames there is an interweaving of plot, characterization, practice (for example, actions used to fight off evil and promote good), and elaborate problem-solving. Children experiment within this forum by taking on new identities and understanding the nature of new cultures. The key to succeeding within the world of computer games is understanding the culture and idiosyncrasies and dispositions of the characters.

Gee highlights important skills students acquire in their use of videogames:

1 active and critical thinking;

2 appreciation and understanding of design;

3 problem-solving skills;

4 principles of semiotics (as in images working with words, with actions, with symbols, with artefacts);

5 identity principles in taking on different personalities and working within their logic;

6 understanding what it means to work within cultural models (that is, models carrying values, beliefs, and so on) (Gee, 2003).

WORKING WITH STUFF

It is the *manner* in which we make texts that signifies our own interpretation. It is, as Kress puts it, the *stuff* we use to make texts which inscribes or embeds our identities into them (Kress, 1997). *Stuff* can range from different fonts, to high-quality paper, to cut-out bits of paper glued onto cardboard, to a child's drawing, to full colour – any material that best suits a text based on the *interest* of the producer. Kress uses the term **materiality** to describe the stuff we use to make a text. Stuff could consist of words and our knowledge of action and gesture in role-play or visuals, and written words combined with our knowledge of characterization and plot in writing a story for class. Importantly, Kress discusses meaning-as-form and form-as-meaning. You cannot have one without the other and when we create texts, meaning and form stand on equal footing.

> ## Questions to consider with children's writing
>
> - In which genre are they working?
> - What is the function of the text?
> - What language or Discourse should they use?
> - How much of their identities, for example, out-of-school interests, should a child bring to a text?
> - Who is the intended audience?
> - What is the format and layout of the text?
> - Where will the text be read?
> - Is the text represented best in print or electronic form?
> - Are the visuals realistic or interpretative?
> - Should they include photographs or illustrations?
> - Should the text be viewed in one, two or three dimensions?

More than ever, the materials we use to make texts are key to understanding texts. A child creating a web page considers what links there will be to other pages; she considers the amount and placement of written text; she considers the colour scheme and the purpose of visuals in the interface; she decides whether to include movement by using Flash or other programs; she decides whether to include sound; she considers the size of the monitor on which the text will be viewed. Collectively, these decisions comprise the materiality of the text and they have everything to do with how we make meaning from a text. We have more choices than ever in our making and reading of texts, which implies that, more than ever, we have to understand and interpret the materiality of texts. In teaching, there is a difference between lecturing with or without overheads versus teaching using PowerPoint. The former teaching method is still an accepted model, but perhaps less stimulating compared with the interactive, visual and oral nature of PowerPoint.

WHAT IS POSSIBLE WITHIN TEXTUAL FORMS?

Often the issue of materiality comes down to the **affordances** and **constraints** of the materials we use. Affordances are the possibilities that a particular form offers a text-maker. Kress asks, what are the affordances of a mode and what are its constraints? Worded differently, what materials give a text greater power and attention and what materials lessen its power and attention? In writing an essay, a student strives to have an academic voice, demonstration of research skills, use of proper and accurate grammar, punctuation, and mechanics and an understanding of style. Understanding and applying the principles of academic writing *affords* opportunities to succeed in school. Whereas not accounting for punctuation, vocabulary and structure *constrains* success in academic writing. As we show in Chapter 6, where a group of students designed a PowerPoint presentation to show to parents at an open evening, if a student designs a web page or develops a PowerPoint presentation, they will have to consider font, use of graphics, amount of written text, summarizing and selecting key points, and on the whole, take account of the *affordances* of text features when creating their presentation. As sign-makers, students have to factor-in the benefit of each material they use. The possibilities open to the student, and the choices they make, in relation to the affordance of each mode have yet to be subject to an assessment regime, but questions of assessment of multimodal choice remain pertinent in our multimodal world.

READING PATH

Texts are no longer straightforward. Electronic texts do not follow a linear path, but instead follow a series of links that lead you into different texts tied but separate from the original one. Take a typical web page. Written parts of the text are often labels for an image or instructions. Sometimes there are sound bites, there is movement in animated text, there are captions at the bottom related to the text but somewhat outside of it, there are hotspots taking us to another site or another page, there is hypertext giving definitions, and so on. All these bits of text move us around the page and we have far more options than we did before. With these texts in mind, we need to re-evaluate our notion of *reading path*.

> **Gunther Kress and Carey Jewitt: Revising our notion of reading path**
>
> Carey Jewitt and Gunther Kress argue that we must attend to the role of new technologies because they are demanding different kinds of skills from our students. They claim that these new forms of communication carry **modes**, which are at one and the same time, visual, tactile, linguistic and graphic, and that these modes carry meanings in the texts. New communicational practices involve image, gesture, movement, music, speech

> and sound effect. Where in the past, students read a text and, although they could look ahead to what will be said or unfold, they followed a standard path, such is not the case with modern texts (Jewitt and Kress, 2003).

Different cultures have made different decisions about reading paths in their writing systems, whether from right to left or from left to right. Multimodal texts open up the question again by allowing the user to choose where you go in a text. With the predominance of technology, computer screens and images frame our use of language. In this way, writing, where it occurs on-screen, is subordinated to the logic of the screen (Kress, 2003). We are far more likely to be aware of headers and footers, of boldface text and of double- versus single-spaced writing on-screen compared to writing handwritten text. We have a visual reflex when we write on-screen.

Reading paths on-screen are not necessarily governed by the whims of the reader but, instead, as frequent users of electronic texts we are socialized into ways or practices of using these texts. Students we teach learn how to move around web pages and use hypertext when they need to by observing others do so, and by experimenting with new media themselves. Students have been socialized into the world of contemporary media. They are far more *disposed* to seeing the screen as a point of reference for strategies of reading. In this way, literacy skills are tied to reading strategies used during computer use (cutting and pasting text, using spell and grammar check, formatting texts); these practices are natural, assumed and tacit.

ACTIVITY

Reading path

Get on the Web and visit three websites.

Chart how you navigate through them.

Write down your path and where it led you.

Then look at a web page in greater detail.

Analyse where written text sits and what visuals do.

What is the logic behind your reading path?

What compelled you to move to another page and did you return to the original one?

HOW DO WE APPLY THIS THEORY TO TEACHING?

On a practical level, within the classroom, children need to understand texts and how texts are put together to use and make for themselves. Texts and the meanings within texts are tied together. If texts are viewed as artefacts, which are made by certain people (for example, child and adult), in certain social contexts, with certain functions in mind they can be explored further.

One activity to try with older students is to consider different newspapers. If you juxtapose three different newspapers you will find that each one is speaking to a certain reader and reflects a certain values. Differences between the three papers materialize in the tone and the style of the writing as much as they materialize in the layout, font and format. The articulation of content and design speaks to a particular person in a particular situation. Like an archaeological artefact, aspects of a text's materiality are clues to who made it, when, how and why.

When teaching, it helps to suggest to students that books are physical, live artefacts with a story and system behind them. By 'live' we mean that people working in a place through a set of practices brought its physical state into being. What does this have to do with teaching literacy? Viewing the texts children use and make in class in this light gives them a far deeper understanding of genre, of design, of editing and of language than restricting literacy to balancing phonics instruction with whole language. On the whole, children understand by doing and by using symbolic practices – whether with image, music or written text – and understanding texts as artefacts of practices facilitates a more meaningful engagement with language.

Vignette: Making comic books in a grade 7 class

In Andras Valezy's grade 7 English class, he taught a comic-book unit. To begin the unit, he asked students to bring to class comic strips, comic books or any other texts that combine pictures and words to tell a story. As a group, they compared the texts and picked features that could be used to differentiate a comic book from other picture books. Then Andras read a comic book to the class. He usually chose X-Men because it dealt with a group of adolescent superheroes that were not accepted by society because of their mutations but were adopted by a professor who helped them to harness their powers. Most students enjoyed the story. They were keen to talk about characterization and plot, and to analyse and critique the stories.

As part of the unit, Andras asked the class to compare X-Men to other media-related spin-offs of the comic-book genre; this included X-Men videogames, cartoons and movies. As their final assignment, students created their own comic book. Some students chose to author and illustrate their work independently. Andras had one group of students who worked together to create a comic book by taking on roles of their characters and using a 35 mm camera to capture images. They finished off the project by adding dialogue to the still shots. Yet another group of students had the idea of filming their comic book once they had finished their assignment.

TEXTS AS TRACES OF SOCIAL PRACTICE

Consider for a moment the texts that you use in your classroom. In all likelihood the types of texts you will see are textbooks in various subject areas; reading centres with picture books or novels, non-fiction texts, perhaps dual-language and community language texts; policy documents such as curriculum documents, special needs and English as an Additional Language (EAL) documents, school policies; posters, maps, student artefacts; binders filled with evaluation forms, assessment tools, and so on. These texts are not only traces of the culture in which you work, traces of you as a teacher with your notion of **pedagogy** and practice, but also traces of various other contexts all sitting in one room with 20 to 30 students. As discussed and illustrated above, texts are traces of people, contexts and implied practices.

When you use a reading scheme it carries within it a specific model of literacy, a specific method of teaching (direct and structured vs more informal), specific literacy practices like guided reading or literature circles, and sometimes even specific readers in mind (for example, an EAL emphasis in a reading scheme).

Textbooks are the product of a long collaborative process amongst publishing teams that bring their own identities and context agendas into books that ultimately guide our understandings of how to teach a discipline. A reading scheme carries ways of teaching, philosophies of literacy *and* literacy practices that should take place – even *where* they should take place (for example, in small groups with different worksheets that students complete at a table). While these practices are taken for granted in classrooms, reading scheme books assume and reflect these practices. The reading scheme book is a text which retain traces of its making, and the identities of the makers are inscribed within the text.

THE READER AND THE WRITER

Reading or meaning-making incites a dialogue between text user and text producer. That is, what we use in making texts is key to our interpretation of meanings *in* texts. In a reading series, we may find stylized illustrations to match the storyline and cultural heritage of authors in a student anthology book; these design features and content themes affect our reading of the text. If EAL students are reading a text *through* illustrations, which often happens, interpretations of the story through illustrations (which is done by the illustrator-designer in publishing companies) are controlling the interpretation of the text.

Reading schemes are unique in that they are usually restricted to classroom use. Rarely do you see scheme books on a shelf in someone's home. As such, they are tied to, and constrained by, schooling practices (for example, paired reading, group reading, independent reading). Reading textbooks therefore carry a genre of schooled literacy and carry their own rites and associations.

ACTIVITY

Tracing practices in your classroom

Take out a reading scheme you use in your classroom. Take a look at the student book and the teacher's resource book. Answer all or some of these questions:

Who is the author?

Who is the publisher?

Can you identify a model of teaching and learning?

How would you use this resource?

How does it inform or guide your teaching?

Does it provide modifications for other student learners?

What is the design of the text?

How does the visual work with the written?

Write a synopsis of how you might use the textbook and some of the practices that would grow out of using it. Describe how you might design the textbook or teacher's resource book differently.

Think about the routines around literacy such as where reading takes place (for example, a carpeted area vs at desks with worksheets). Usually, reading programmes like the *Oxford Reading Tree* carry routines and familiar visuals of characters like Kipper with them that control what takes place and when. When reading schemes are aligned with policy initiatives like the National Literacy Hour in Britain, you find that texts guide literacy events and practices that take place within classroom spaces. Publishers inter-weave dominant models of literacy in documents like the National Literacy Strategy Framework for Teaching (DfEE, 1998) with their own models of literacy in reading schemes. They do so because they are in the business of selling books and hence they have to embed curricular mandates into their texts. The important point here is that these sorts of texts are central to how and what gets taught during literacy time.

Teachers and students would enrich literacy lessons, and perhaps even their texts and practices, if they analysed embedded assumptions in texts and authorial voices as traces of not only an author's perspective, but also a publisher's/producer's perspective; for example, facing questions like:

- What has gone into producing this text?

- How does the interface between written and visual text affect text content?

Curricular documents should face the same scrutiny, being aware as practitioners:

- Who wrote them?

- Who reviewed them?

- How do they want lessons or units to be used (religiously, dip in and out)?

Every text we use carries traces of practices. To know these practices is to empower our teaching.

Such research helps us as literacy teachers to attend to such factors as:

1   how and when texts are used;
2   practices around texts;
3   where reading scheme practices take place within the geography of the room;
4   traces of publisher-produced models in literacy events; and
5   how teachers mediate text content.

LITERACY AS A MULTIMODAL PRACTICE

One of the key themes in Chapter 1 was literacy as a social practice. Children not only communicate across culture, but as stated earlier, in *relation to* cultures. Culture can be seen as an active concept. For children, a primary means of engaging with different cultures lies in using new, changing, global forms of communication like the Internet and email. In classrooms and in homes, children interact with the local and the global in their use of the Internet, videogames, texting, emailing, and so on. They use these technologies, but do they understand their meanings beyond a response to the stimuli, the visual and the tactile? Modes rarely exist alone but instead are combined with animation, with movement, with gesture and with words. This is due to the exponential increase in the role of the visual.

Kress and Van Leeuwen: Grammar of visual design

Gunther Kress and Theo Van Leeuwen, in *Reading Images: The Grammar of Visual Design*, demonstrate that visual text has a grammar of its own which can work in synchronization and at odds with written text. An example in speech that Kress and Van Leeuwen supply is a child saying 'This is a heavy hill'. Although the child is constrained by not having the word 'steep', he focuses on particular aspects of climbing a hill and uses an available form to do so. A child uses available resources, as they put it, to make a text or express a thought. The basis of this thought comes from experiences with texts and speech they have acquired and stored away. They focus on the 'interest' of the sign-maker as pivotal in creating the text (Kress and Van Leeuwen, 1996).

Vignette: Reading images

In Anne Burke's secondary classroom in St John's, Newfoundland, she uses a multimodal approach to deliver her history curriculum. In her class, students explore history through a number of drama structures using art as a medium. In order for students to explore character more deeply in a role-play, students are taught how artists convey meanings through artistic elements of design. Anne uses a number of pictures that explore a period of World War II. In using a multimodal approach, students are introduced to the use of picture books not only as an object that conveys meaning

▶

through text, but also through illustrations. Anne asks students to consider how picture-book illustrations allow them to extend their meaning-making of plot and interpretation of a character's thoughts, feelings and emotions. For this unit, Anne invites students to consider how an illustrator uses artistic elements of design (line, colour, texture and shape) to convey the narrative of the story.

In the case of picture books, the narrative nature of picture books invites readers or viewers to see how artistic elements act as a form of visual communication. In many picture books, illustrators show the relationship a character has with other characters or further extends a character's intentions in the plot through movement, performance and gesture. An illustrator's choice for a character's clothing and the colour of the pictured dress can highlight the socio-economic status of characters. The choices an illustrator makes provide clues to the reader and viewer as to how the character may be feeling or as an explanation for their actions.

For Anne, the most intriguing thing about the class was discovering that students actually did draw upon the image-making techniques of the illustrator. Students used the interpretations of the artistic elements and redefined them as their own. In particular, it was evident in their use of colour. Students used different symbolic associations of the use of colour to describe what emotions the characters in the illustrations were feeling. For example, the colour 'red' suggested danger or passion. When reflecting on using a multimodal approach to teaching history, Anne said, 'through a multimodal approach, I can show students how the use of "written text" and "spoken text" are not the only modes that can yield desirable responses in a classroom. A study of the illustrator's use of artistic elements of design in picture books helps students increase their visual literacy'.

Some key principles

There are key principles we think about in our making and reading of texts:

1   The idea behind the text (for example, a manual explaining how a washing machine works).

2   The relationship with the viewer (for example, a consumer with a warranty who wants to know the parts or be able to fix the machine).

3   What the genre demands of the text (for example, active verbs and paragraphs with lots of visuals to support written texts and phone numbers in case they cannot sort out the problem).

Kress and Van Leeuwen offer a grammar of visual design to demonstrate that the visual is (often) a separate medium of expression with its own rules and conventions. They address a variety of texts from children's picture books to social studies textbooks to advertisements to works of art to sculpture. Kress and Van Leeuwen provide a framework for visual analysis that we can use to interpret texts (Kress and Van Leeuwen, 1996).

One of the most powerful vehicles for the visual is to establish a relationship between the producer and the reader. They discuss how producers are cognizant and write for and to a model reader through their choices in language and in multimodality.

Over the course of an interview with a senior editor at Ginn Publishers in the UK, Rowsell discussed the role of visual communication in children's books. When asked about the role of the visual, the editor maintained:

> *The visual has an increasingly important role. We are increasingly putting more emphasis into things like typography. Typography is something you have to get right with big books ... We spend a lot of time briefing artists on what texts should look like. We stress the sort of detail that can get missed, like we do not want kids in the books to be in spotless clothing all of the time ...* (Rowsell, 2000: 201).

Clearly, in light of new technologies, there is a greater consciousness of the visual as carrying its own informational and ideological potential.

ACTIVITY

The grammar of visual design

Think about the list of key principles to think of when 'reading' an image. In the UK, a booklet, **More than Words: Multimodal Texts in the Classroom**, invites teachers to focus on the following questions when looking at children's multimodal texts:

> How can we describe what children know and can do as shown in their multimodal texts – in this case drawing plus writing?

> What are the implications for classroom practice: how can teachers help pupils develop and extend their control of different modes? (QCA, 2004)

The booklet highlighted how children's choices about layout features such as colour, font size and style, choice of language and overall design in combining words and images all worked to create different ways in which the texts were read and received (QCA, 2004:18–19).

The booklet left teachers with the question, 'What does getting better at multimodal presentation look like?'

TEXTS WE USE

The texts we use on a daily basis inside classrooms and in our homes are clues to our culture, our values, our belief systems, even what carries currency in our local worlds. The texts we use in our classrooms are at one and the same time local and global. Textbooks, for example, depict our local worlds but usually with a global overlay. Publishers with global partnerships often recycle content in other contexts but put a local overlay on the same texts. For example, a spelling series developed in Canada with American and British spelling might serve as a template for a spelling series developed in Britain with British spellings and local terminology.

Gemma Moss: Junior-age boys and non-fiction books

In Gemma Moss's work, she observed boys as they perused non-fiction texts. These studies were part of a series of interlinked research projects that analysed literacy events with boys. Moss looked at how reading becomes culturally and socially shaped through interactions between people during literacy events. Moss considered a Dorling Kindersley approach to design, which one can see in such series as the *Eyewitness Guides*. She noted that the series was constructed around photographs of objects, which are large and spread over two pages (defying publishing rules around a book's gutter). The pictures dominate more space than the written text and are placed centrally. The junior-age boys in Moss's studies were drawn to these books above others largely due to the uniqueness of their design. Part of the affordances, as discussed earlier, that these texts offered is the capacity for weaker readers to steer their way around them without being hindered by the written word. These sorts of texts give some boys the confidence to move forward in print (Moss, 1999; 2003).

ACTIVITY

Texts to practice

Revisit the list of texts children use (given at the start of this chapter) and beside each one, list some of the modes you would find.

Is one mode featured over another (for example, in a newspaper the written mode is **usually** featured more than in magazines)?

Is the text written for a particular audience?

If so, who is the audience?

What style are the illustrations (for example, graphic in cartoons)?

How do the visuals relate back to the audience and function of the text?

How do the words and pictures work together?

Why is this mode featured?

How does this mode work to create the meaning?

Make a list of texts that we might use in a day. Think about this, and write about visual communication in the text.

THE MEDIUM IS THE MESSAGE

What does work on multimodality mean for literacy research? What you can draw from such work is to relate literacy practices and events going on in a particular site and situate them within the global. For example, if you were conducting a research study on junior-age boys' use of new media at home and at school, you would ask such questions as:

- What texts are they reading or using?

- What are they using them for?

- Where are they using them?

- Are texts made locally or in other contexts?

- Do characters in the texts relate to their own culture and lived experience, or are they tied to another culture?

- What is the difference between texts they use at home and at school?

- Is one set of texts tied more to local culture than the other?

If more attention is paid to what children read and write, when, where, how and why, then we would have much more of an awareness of how children think and understand language today. One way of doing this is to watch children in their out-of-school literacy practices. Observing children navigating a videogame, or making a **weblog**, gives us clues as to how an understanding of multimodality aids thinking and communicating skills.

REFLECTION ON MULTIMODAL LITERACY

When I walk through classrooms to visit student teachers or to meet with classroom teachers, I consistently remark at the buzz of activity in primary classrooms and, what is more, at the carousel of activities and attendant texts. There are non-fiction books on topics such as farmers or frogs and toads; there are picture books by Michael Rosen and Robert Munsch; there are posters featuring language items like spelling tips, personal dictionaries and punctuation marks; there are visuals showing the growth cycle of plants; not to mention a bevy of activity around the computer centre. Texts, in short, have everything to do with literacy – catalysing, maintaining and mobilizing the reading process. Knowing what they do – how they are written, who they are written by and for, how they were made and why they were made – leads us that much closer to educating children on what it means to be literate. There have never been as many texts as there are today and never in as many modes. Each mode carrying with it a different set of assumptions.

When children read they are doing far more than decoding print – they are acknowledging font, appreciating layout, choosing one design over another, engaging with **avatars**, they are using the visual in meaningful ways. These texts span all disciplines and topics, and are in constant use. As new or experienced teachers or teacher educators, our tacit use implies an understanding but does not necessarily mean that we appreciate their role as educating our students and imparting ideologies and values. As educators we should teach the role and significance of multimodality, and how texts are artefacts that carry processes, as made by people with interests in materiality and as made up of modes.

Think back for a moment to Angie's group of boys, to Andras's interactive language activities and to Anne's awareness of the visual and multimodal in reading and writing, and how each one of these teachers built on their theory and practice to teach language in a meaningful and contemporary light. Their vision informs this book and helps us grasp what it means to use, understand and teach the modern text.

CONCLUSION

We cannot afford to ignore the communicational landscape our students find themselves in. If we harness it, and tie it to literacy learning, its potential is huge. However, we might not see how the visual adds to literacy, it is already embedded within literacy, within the landscape of communication our students engage in. It is our challenge to capture its flows and ebbs, and to develop a dialogue with our students, across the flow of web pages, instant messaging, texting, emailing and the graphic novels and comic books of our students, we will develop a literacy curricula that matches and recognizes our changing world.

Part of the challenge is to see how we can learn from our students and at the same time stretch their understandings in a multimodal communicative landscape. What would a better multimodal text look like? How can we credit the complex interaction between words and pictures so that both are recognized as salient and bringing meaning to each other? By considering words with pictures, how are the words different? These questions concern us as educators, and remain with us, as we bring our students' changing communicative practices into our classrooms.

CHAPTER 3

Children's Texts Go to School

Vignette: A shoebox filled with artefacts

A child is given a shoebox by her teacher. The children and the teacher jointly compose a letter to accompany it, which asks parents to support the child in filling the box with objects and artefacts that might provide a motivational stimulus for writing. The child goes home and collects her items over the school holiday. She assembles a variety of objects including Disney models [from McDonald's], pictures of flowers, whistles, toy cars, a pair of sunglasses and a book, Farmyard Tales Christmas. She takes these into school and explains how she is planning to use them in her stories. She then writes her story. This story is a much stronger story than the teacher has seen previously. The child has connected up her home–school worlds through artefacts (Feiler et al., in press).

KEY THEMES IN THE CHAPTER

- *Research on home–school literacy*
- *Rethinking boundaries between home and school*
- *What counts as literacy learning at home?*
- *Bringing home to school*

INTRODUCTION

Imagine that you are in a classroom – teaching or observing or working at your desk – and you see one of your students reading a comic book or drawing/making a picture of a bird instead of working on his mathematics or language activities. At first, you might think that he is avoiding doing work. However, digging deeper, you find that he does not understand the task at hand and reverts back to what he can do and what interests him. How would you react in this situation? Could it be a situation when you can build on what he knows and likes in the lesson at hand or another aspect of your lesson? What can be observed is that this child is at the interface between group knowledge (that is, what his fellow students are doing) and individual knowledge (that is, what he carries with him).

In this chapter the focus will be on how children's experience of literacy at home interacts with literacy at school. Drawing on recent research on children's literacy at home, the chapter will provide you with tools to support students' learning in relation to the wealth of experience they bring to school. It will see out-of-school literacies as being an important site for students to develop their literacy, and it will bring this perspective to the chapter. This chapter will then look at what happens when children's texts go to school.

The chapter will combine a focus on current research, with examples of how home–school literacies can be considered in relation to classrooms. In order to look at home and school literacy, researchers have come up with an important way of distinguishing between the two. Rather than see the literacy children do at school as the only form of literacy, researchers have identified the literacy children do at school as, **schooled literacy**, tied to the school domain. By contrast out-of-school literacy, which can take place in many diverse sites, including homes, community centres and street corners, is sometimes very different.

Teaching and learning take place in many spaces, and our students will absorb information unexpectedly and in different places, for example, at home, in play schemes, clubs or activity centres. When students are in the classroom they will sometimes pay attention and sometimes not. Our students' attention and interest will ebb and flow in and out of our teaching. By bridging a gap between home and school, we allow them in far more.

Researchers have used words such as domain and **site** to look at home and school literacy. A *domain* is the sphere where a literacy practice originally was created and used. A *site* is the place where the literacy practice is actually engaged with. For example, homework is an activity where the domain is school, but the site is home. The chart below describes how homework can be seen in relation to domain and site.

Domain	Site
School	Home

This chapter provides an overview of the home–school literacy debate, engaging in current research and bringing the perspective of the school closer to the perspective of the home.

WHAT DO WE COUNT AS LITERACY?

When children compose in the classroom, their composing process is accompanied by play, gesture, drawing and talk. Students may use *drama*, *photography*, *multimedia* and *information and communication technology* (ICT) to communicate meaning. In this chapter, literacy is seen as one of a number of communicative practices children engage in. Attention will be given to drawings, model-making, gesture and talk which children bring to their literacy practices.

In home and community contexts, many researchers have looked at how children engage in a number of communicative practices at the same time – perhaps listening to a CD while writing a diary, or text-messaging with friends while doing homework. A child may be on one website to chat with friends, while doing homework on another screen. Or, a child may be playing a console game and find tips on a chatline or website (a bit like cheat sheets) on how to move to the next section of their game.

Therefore, when discussing children's out-of-school literacies, a wider range of communicative practices is drawn upon. This means that this chapter (like Chapter 2) will take account of multimodality. It will also take account of the discussions on how texts can be located in local and global contexts. In this chapter, children's texts will be seen as **crossing** sites, moving into different domains and changing as they do so.

Vignette: Donnington race track

In a family literacy class, as part of a county-wide literacy initiative which supported creativity in family learning, a 4-year-old child brought a multi-modal artefact (see Figure 3.1) to the class that he had done at home the previous week. This was a sheet of paper with cut-out cars glued onto it. In this class, students took a 'backpack' home with materials for drawing, scissors, glue and paper. The backpack was a rucksack filled with materials to encourage creativity with parents at home. The child, who lived with his grandmother, drew a picture of the local racetrack, using cars cut out from a catalogue found at home. He had visited the racetrack previously with his father. The drawing was an image of the track, with the cars placed alongside the track. He was going to give the artefact to his Dad who was coming to see him that evening. The artefact was used in the group and the child told the story, with his grandmother, of his visit to the races (Pahl, 2004a).

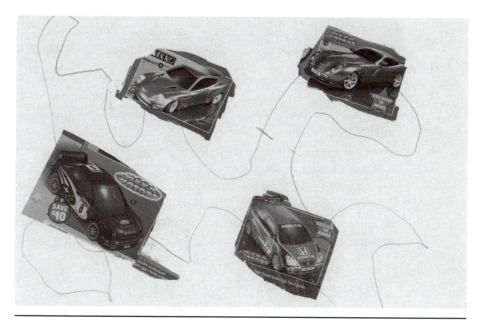

Figure 3.1 Donnington race track

In the vignette, the importance of attending to the wider communicative practices of children can be seen. This image is one which can be identified with 'home' but it crossed sites and went to school. The image of *children's texts crossing sites* is important in this chapter.

Anne Haas Dyson: Recontextualizing texts

A piece of theory which helps us understand what happens when children's text-making goes to school is **recontextualization**. This word has been used to describe the movement of children's texts across sites from one domain to another. Anne Haas Dyson uses this word to describe how children take texts or practices from one domain, and move them across sites, mixing them up as they do so (Dyson, 2003). When children's texts cross boundaries they can be recontextualized into the new setting. The idea of recontextualization that is, moving a piece of writing or drawing which was done in one context, to another context, and embedding it in a different discursive space, is important when considering how children's texts cross sites. These issues can be applied to any setting: school, college or community centre.

Returning to the Donnington race track example, home–school crossings can be seen like this:

Home	School	Home	School	Home
Donnington racetrack – going to see it with his Dad	Encouragement to draw by being given materials	Drawing the Donnington racetrack	Showing the picture at school	Giving the picture to his Dad that evening

At each crossing point, an idea was transformed. In some cases it was recontextualized. That is, the context changed and the child gave a different oral story around the text. The initial experience of going to the racetrack, plus the drawing materials from the project, gave the child the means of making a meaningful text, one that became part of family narratives.

WHAT CAN HOME LITERACY LOOK LIKE?

In this chapter the focus is on home literacies, and then the movement into school. The links between children's text-making at home and at school will be explored. This makes the chapter different from some perspectives on home and school, which consider how school literacy can best be supported at home. When home literacy is described, it often looks very different from school. A child in one research study on home literacy practices wrote emails to her mother, while struggling with reading at school

(Carrington and Luke, 2003). Another child listened to music on her personal CD player while working on a scrap book and reading books on a car journey (Hinchman et al., 2004). Another traces the outline of his home country, Turkey, with his mother's prayer beads (Pahl, 2002). These real-life instances of children's home communicative practices look different from school but are all practices that we can draw on when working with students in school settings.

ACTIVITY

Domains and sites

Think of a literacy practice you engage with which crosses sites. For example, you may collect papers from your workplace to take home.

Describe each text in relation to its site and domain.

Where the domain and the site are different, consider whether the nature of the literacy practice changes as it crosses sites.

RESEARCH ON HOME–SCHOOL LITERACY

Research on home–school literacy has come from a number of disciplines including psychology, anthropology and sociolinguistics. It has focused on a variety of areas, including the ways parents can help their children at school, the ways in which home literacy practices have affected children's literacy at school, and the ways in which home and school can be joined up, through family literacy programmes or other specific ways of supporting parents help their children. Much of this research is underpinned by a belief that children's literacy comes from home, and *the home is where children learn much of their literacy skills*. Most of the research also recognizes the importance of parents in supporting their children.

However, while some studies regard the home literacy practices of parents and children as being worthy of research, others have focused on how parents can adapt their behaviour to support children's literacy learning at school, and have focused less on the resources parents bring to literacy. Literacy practices, on the other hand, may not be the same at home as at school. Many parents speak other languages than the language of the school. Many homes contain different cultural resources from those of schools. For example, many schools do not draw on children's popular culture, and do not see this as a resource when teaching children to write; at home, the word 'Barbie' may be a frequently written word. At school, images are less salient. At home, children may watch television, draw and play-act with more freedom. Parents may bring in their stories and their worlds to children's text-making. There is more latitude for subjectivities and identities in a home space compared with a school space. This is a new area for research, and offers exciting opportunities to engage with children's out-of-school literacy worlds.

This discussion links with a way of conceptualizing home literacy practices which recognizes what homes bring to literacy. This approach acknowledges how every home brings with it identities, dispositions, stories, objects, artefacts, memories, languages and resources. This implies a *wealth* model of literacy by which families' **cultural capital** can be drawn upon when planning schooled literacy activities.

Luis Moll: Funds of knowledge

The wealth model has been linked to a number of theories and approaches. One is from Moll, who worked with Mexican-American parents (Moll et al., 1992). He used the term **funds of knowledge** to describe the cultural heritage and concepts parents bring to their children's literacies. Moll's work has influenced many educational researchers who have considered what homes bring to children's literacy practices. The wealth model often draws on detailed ethnographic work in homes to identify the resources families bring to literacy.

However, many educators try to bridge the gap between home and school, to meet parents on their own territory and listen to their experience and resources. In this chapter, we build on that model and provide an account of home literacy practices which values what parents bring to literacy. The next section will begin by considering research on children's schooled literacy practices, and how they can be supported at home.

CHILDREN'S SCHOOLED LITERACY PRACTICES

When a child arrives at school, the child begins school with a wealth of knowledge about the world to support his or her learning. Within school, this knowledge is translated into a focus on learning, and particularly a focus on literacy. Schooled literacy concentrates on lettered, alphabetic literacy and its acquisition. Drawing on models of literacy development from psychologists such as Lev Vygotsky and researchers in the field of emergent literacy such as Marie Clay, teachers work with children to foster their reading and writing skills (Clay, 1975; Vygotsky, 1978). Books are at the heart of this process.

When researchers considered how parents could support their children at home, the reading of books became the centre of the strategies parents could be given to support their children's literacy. The *book bag* is one example of this practice, whereby a child is sent home with a book to read. This is accompanied by a reading record, in order for the parent to communicate how the reading had gone.

Other ideas include *storysacks*, which are bags with a book, and play items and artefacts connected to the story which children can do at home. Recent initiatives in bridging home and school have extended the storysacks idea to include *backpacks*. Inside the backpack are paper, pens, colouring pencils and writing equipment so that children can write stories at home and send them to school (Pahl, 2004).

Many of these ideas come from research. One of the very first studies on home–school literacy support by parents was a study by Tizard and Hughes who looked in more detail at home–school support (Tizard and Hughes, 1984). They found that parents who supported their children's reading at home did better at school. This study led to many developments in schools, including the use of book bags, and links between home and school being strengthened.

Another key initiative which supported children's schooled learning and parents' own literacy skills was **family literacy**. This initiative takes many forms, the chief is activities which involve literacy with both children and their parents. Many schools encourage family literacy classes on site, and family literacy programmes are popular as offering a fun, supportive environment for children and parents to learn together. In the UK an evaluation for the Basic Skills Agency's Family Literacy Programme, *Family Literacy Works* (Brooks et al., 1996) concluded that family literacy programmes offered parents and children a strong foundation for literacy.

HOME AND SCHOOL TOGETHER

Yet, many of these initiatives focused mostly on what children learned at school, and how parents could support that. A different way of conceptualizing how parents could support children's literacy was the *ORIM framework*, developed by Peter Hannon, Cathy Nutbrown and Jo

Weinberger at the University of Sheffield. This gave parents a framework to use with their children which could be translated into literacy support for children's schooled literacy. Parents could provide:

> **Opportunities** for their children's literacy development (trips, visits, shopping, materials for writing, drawing, books, opportunities for play).
>
> **Recognition** of their literacy practices (explicitly valuing what children do, and listening to them talking, playing and writing).
>
> **Interaction** with children to develop their literacy (such as spelling out words children want to write, looking at letter/sound names, helping children spell a word).
>
> **Model** their own literacy practices (reading signs, directions, instructions, packaging, print in the environment, writing notes, letters, shopping lists, reading newspapers) (Hannon and Nutbrown, 1997).

When seen as a way of crediting home literacy practices, the ORIM framework has a powerful impact on the home–school literacy crossing. Recent evaluation of the use of the ORIM framework has also been very positive, particularly amongst teachers, who used it to discover how much parents were supporting their children's literacy at home (Hannon and Nutbrown, 1997). The Raising Early Achievement in Literacy (REAL) project collaborated with school teachers in developing a home-focused programme, based on the ORIM framework, that was tried with over 80 families with preschool children. The programme included home visits by the teachers. Emerging findings indicate that the project was welcomed by families and that it had an impact on children's literacy development, compared with controls (Hannon and Nutbrown, 2001).

Many of these different ways of supporting children's literacy rest on studies which showed what children were doing at home before they came to school. A significant study was Wells's *The Meaning Makers* (Wells, 1986) which followed children from a wide range of socio-economic backgrounds and their speaking, reading and writing at home and at school. Wells provided a key part of the home–school puzzle when the findings emerged that children from low socio-economic backgrounds engaged in a rich plethora of literacy practices at home.

As seen in Heath's (1983) study of children's literacy and language practices in three different communities, the arguments began to build up about the importance of recognizing children's specific literacy and language practices at home. Heath's study showed that in some homes the interaction between parents and children had certain qualities, which may not be the same as 'schooled' ways of interacting. Michaels's (1986) study of first graders' oral interactions at school also found that particular children, in the case of her research, African-American children, had ways of speaking which were not fully recognized in the 'schooled' domain.

Oral communication in different cultures was closely studied by researchers. They found that different communities, following Heath's insight, spoke and communicated differently. For example, Hymes (1996) looked at oral narrative skills in America's different communities. He argued that we, as educators, need to listen to the patterns of storytelling these communities brought to the study of narrative (Hymes, 1996).

Rebecca Rogers: A mismatch between home and school

An ethnographic study by Rebecca Rogers (2003) also showed how one African-American family had strong and diverse literacy practices, which were not duplicated in the schooled domain, but were unrecognized by school educators. In her study of the Treaders, an African-American family, many literacy practices were observed at home, but the daughter was considered special education material, and despite her struggles to remain in mainstream education, was not seen as mainstream. In Rogers's account, this was linked to a mismatch between home and school literacy practices, with home literacy practices not being valued by the school.

In the field of multilingual literacies, there have been a number of illuminating studies looking at how children's literacy develops at home and then is supported at school. In Charmian Kenner's *Home Pages* (2000) she described how Billy, aged 3 years, 5 months, was immersed in a *literacy world* which included his country of origin, Thailand, his local community, including the Thai temple he attended, his school, where his mother helped out, his home, and his own interests and activities at home including cartoons and videos he liked to watch (Kenner, 2000). By mapping Billy's literacy world, Kenner could see where and how literacy activities blended with school literacy activities, and where they were separate.

Eve Gregory and Ann Williams: Siblings and literacy development
■

In a study by Eve Gregory and Ann Williams, of children growing up in the East End of London, siblings were important in developing children's schooled literacy practices. Through the familiar activity of 'playing school' younger siblings learned the rhythms and sounds of school literacy activities. Gregory and Williams used the phrase **syncretic literacy** to describe how children took ways of doing literacy from school, and blended them with ways of doing literacy at home, or in the mosque school many children attended. They observed how children in community classes (mosque school) often had to repeat after the teacher, whereas this pattern is reversed in the English classroom. At home, children merged and blended these different patterns of interaction when they played school (Gregory and Williams, 2000).

In a study of Bangladeshi women in Birmingham, UK, by Adrian Blackledge the particular literacy practices of the mothers were not valued at school, and were not drawn upon in classroom activities. Blackledge made the following key suggestions for educators who wish to connect up school and home when working with children and parents who speak other languages than English (Blackledge, 2000). Schools can:

a. *make concerted efforts to communicate with families in their home languages*
b. *make explicit their understanding that community literacies, including oral literacies, contribute to children's learning*
c. *affirm families' cultural identity within and beyond the curriculum*
d. *make genuine attempts to involve parents in their children's education, including at policy-making level.* (Blackledge, 2000: 69)

Blackledge is clear that there is an imbalance of power between home and school, particularly when women from different cultural identities do not have their own language recognized in the mainstream school system. These parents valued their spoken Sylheti language and their community language of Bengali, but did not see those languages recognized in the school their children attended. This disjuncture rendered the women powerless in their concern to support their children's learning (Blackledge, 2000: 68). This study shows how the coming together of home and school is sometimes difficult in the face of a misunderstanding of linguistic identities. This brings us to look at what children do with literacy at home. How can literacy be conceptualized at home? What does it look like and what form does it take?

CHILDREN'S OUT-OF-SCHOOL LITERACY PRACTICES

Children's out-of-school literacies have been divided into two types of literacy practice. In an article by Michele Knobel and Colin Lankshear a distinction was made between those literacies which look like school literacy such as story-reading, name-writing, print awareness and completing school homework, and those literacies which do not look like school literacy and, often, will not be tolerated in school (Knobel and Lankshear, 2003). These could include literacy practices that are in response to popular culture, or those which are too far away from 'schooled literacy practices', such as drawing or model-making. Linking visual communicative practices to forms of literacy such as writing or speaking and listening is key to understanding **out-of-school literacy practices**. Part of the difficulty of looking at out-of-school literacies is that often they are conducted not by one child, but by grandparents, by siblings or across different groupings in families (Rashid and Gregory, 1997), a finding which Rashid and Gregory's work demonstrates.

ACTIVITY

Listing home literacy practices

Think back to your own experience of growing up.

What did you do at home with literacy?

Make a list of all the activities you remember doing when you were at home.

Include drawing and oral story-telling in your list.

Then make a list of all the activities connected to literacy you did at school.

Draw a line between the activities which connect up in some way.

Which activities are different?

Why is that?

A study by Denny Taylor, published in 1983, documented the rich vein of literacy practices in homes. Taylor's detailed ethnographic studies of American families, suggested how parents brought a strong diversity of literacies which incorporated different identities and narratives. Taylor argued that these narratives should be used to tell schools how to teach literacy (Taylor, 1983).

In many research studies, there has been evidence that has backed up Taylor's findings and has helped educators appreciate the complex literacy practices children engage in at home. For example, Heath's study of the literacy practices of two different communities in the Carolinas helped us understand different patterns in literacy practices from school patterns (Heath, 1983). There have been fewer studies of children's text-making at home. Kenner's study of **bilingual** children revealed many different sorts of texts being produced by children at home, including word searches, cards and letters (Kenner, 2000). Studies of children's popular culture and literacy found that many children responded to the videos and games they played with, incorporating dance, songs and stories (Marsh and Thompson, 2001). In this chapter, we look at how children's texts develop and change as they go to school. How do they start out, at home, and what happens to them when they go to school?

Vignette: home–school texts crossing sites

This example comes from a study of a Turkish child, Fatih. Fatih was 5 when he was observed at home and at school. His mother, Elif, was Turkish, and had come to the UK from Turkey when she was a teenager to be married. Elif had another child, Hanif, 8. Fatih was having some difficulties with school and was only attending part-time. Elif, Fatih and Hanif lived in a public housing estate in a busy street in North London. Fatih liked to draw, model and make birds at home (Figure 3.2). He also made bird models at school, and was observed in the classroom pretending to be a bird. He used model materials to make birds, and frequently drew or made birds at home and in the family literacy class he attended. He described how he loved chickens, and when he visited his home village, he liked to chase the chickens. The meaning of the bird slowly became clear. Elif was stroking the head of her other son, Hanif, saying 'little bird'. 'Bird?' I said. 'Yes' she said. 'I call them "Bird", "Kus" in Turkish' she said. As the research study progressed, over a two-year period, I watched how Fatih extended his interest in birds across the two sites of home and school.

Figure 3.2 Bird made at home

HOME AND SCHOOL AS LINKED

Fatih clearly kept his interest in birds across the two sites, and even developed the bird theme when at school (Figure 3.3). This linking between home and school has been noted as a key theme for researchers. Both Hull and Schultz (2002) and Street and Street (1991) have commented on how it is important to look at the continuities between home and school, rather than the discontinuities.

In this example, the cross-over between home and school can be seen in the form of Fatih's bird-making practices. This episode shows how texts become artefacts that acquire meanings across sites. By understanding that process, the nature of the home–school boundary can also be rethought. While it is perceived by parents and teachers as a point for separation, the school–home border can be bridged. Fatih was able to duplicate text-making at home and at school successfully. Texts operate as both external artefacts, but as 'tools of identity', they bridge gaps (Holland et al., 2001). Text-making was one constant Fatih had between home and school. In both spaces he had access to paper, pens and scissors. By making texts across sites, he is able to make the bird fly into the classroom.

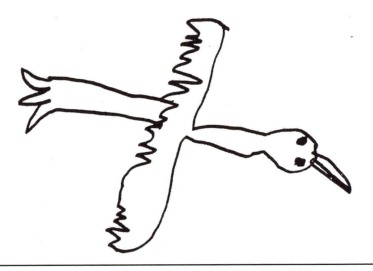

Figure 3.3 Fatih's flying bird made at school

As a research area, the study of texts across sites has implications for how the home–school boundary is bridged. By tracking text-making across sites, home and school become places where rather than different activities being possible, the same activity is possible. The child gains the concept of bird-making wholly from neither site, but blends and mixes techniques of production gained from both home and school.

SYNCRETIC LITERACY PRACTICES

Syncretism is a useful term to describe the taking on of a number of different sociocultural influences in order to produce new, hybrid forms (Duranti and Ochs, 1996). Duranti and Ochs investigated how Samoan families, settled in California, blended and mixed practices from Samoa with the new schooled practices encountered in California. For example, they drew on literacy practices from school, but mixed them with ways of doing things in the home which came from Samoa.

Many texts produced by children have this quality of holding different cultural identities. Millard (2003) described how one boy introduced into an adventure story pictorial narrative, the character of a devil man who had 'come from one Sikh boy's memories of shared stories told to him by his mother' (Millard 2003: 6). Children commonly mix culturally infused stories into their own richly blended narratives.

Vignette: Out-of-school literacy and the 73 bus

It was the spring term in a small, year 1 urban school in London. The children had been sitting in a large group reading 'Humpty Dumpty'. Their teacher had asked them to construct their own versions of this rhyme. The group wrote:

Humpty Dumpty sat on the bus

Humpty Dumpty had a great fuss

All the King's horses and all the King's men couldn't

Make Humpty Dumpty cool down again.

In the group exercise the teacher had drawn a bus, in red, with Humpty Dumpty sitting in it looking cross. I watched Deji as he filled in his sheet with his writing and drawing of the verse on separate sheets (Figure 3.4). Deji followed the group writing almost to the letter. However, at 12.00 he was still frantically 'colouring in'. What was he colouring in and why? He was colouring in a bus using red. He was adding the number 73. In doing so, he located his home and school within a community, the community in North London which is dominated by the 73 bus, the only known means of transport to get from where he lived to that particular school. Deji used this bus every day of his life to go to school. Some time later, I was sitting on the 73 bus when I noticed Deji and his brother sitting in front of me.

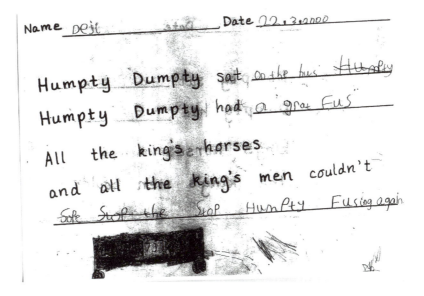

Figure 3.4 73 bus

By drawing his out-of-school experience, but transferring it to a school context, Deji has recontextualized his out-of-school experience, and put it into a nursery rhyme at school.

LITERACY LEARNING IN AND OUT OF SCHOOL

Perhaps it is timely to think how we can draw together our students' in and out-of-school literacy practices. In a recent study by Schultz of students' out-of-school literacy practices young people used writing to make sense of their lives, and the worlds around them during their school years (Schultz, 2002). How could this kind of writing be used in school?

> ### *Vignette: Stories of global migration*
>
> *Clair Marsh, based at CETS, Croydon, London, teaches a Family Literacy class for bilingual parents in a school. The parents brought stories from their own childhoods in different parts of the world to tell their children. The children were aged between 5 and 11 years old. These stories were re-told and then translated by parents and children together, becoming dual texts for ongoing use. Using the characters and focal points of the stories they made puppets and drew pictures which were used to tell the stories in videoed mini-productions. At this stage the stories were quite 'raw' and the children dominated in the storytelling. In the second phase of the project, the group worked on different ways of developing their stories. They added or increased adjectives, rhyming words or alliteration and learned about facial expressions, dramatic gesture and storytelling skills. They looked at the use of musical instruments and additional props to enhance their stories. Together, the parents and children revisited their original stories, enriched them and prepared for a second videoing. A comparison could then be made between the two productions. The second recording illustrated the progression of both parents and children. The stories were now more interesting, parents and children showed greater co-operation and desire to work together, the parents in particular gained confidence and several children showed an increased level of respect for their parents. This activity both valued the parents' home cultures and supported children's literacy in school.*

How can educators draw on these examples to improve their practice? In much of the work on children's out-of-school literacies, there is a recognition of how children blend a number of different forms, and draw on different ways of making meaning when they make texts. Dyson calls this process 'remix' and applies it in her work to the children she observed who mixed rap songs and nursery rhymes in their out-of-school practices (Dyson, 2003). In this chapter we have looked at the following examples of literacy practices:

- *syncretic* literacy practices, for example, where Fatih wrote English 'bird', drawing on his school experience of reading *The Ugly Duckling*, but also on his home experiences of Turkey, with the Turkish 'Kus';

- *hybrid* literacy, for example, where Deji described the 73 bus in the same text as the Humpty Dumpty poem, thus bringing together two different traditions and using writing and drawing;

- *multimodal* literacy, as we saw in Deji's text, the meaning is in both the drawing of the bus and the writing.

Can you find examples of these concepts in your own classroom?

In this chapter, texts have been the focus in looking at how children can link up home and school. Eve Bearne writes that, 'Rethinking literacy requires a pedagogy which can accommodate to children's situated text experience brought from the everyday world of communications and relate this both to the schooled literacy of the classroom situation and to the institutional practices which shape current practice.' (Bearne, 2003: 102). This means that when we think about children's text-making, we consider all the influences that come into their lives. In this chapter, we suggest that children's text-making at home and at school needs to become more 'joined up'.

THIRD SPACE THEORY

One way to think about home and school is to consider a **third space** where children can write out their home experiences. This could be, for example, a space where children can choose what they write about, or bring in artefacts from home to write about. The third space has been used to describe the in-between literacy practices of prisoners, who write to the outside world drawing on an 'in-between' space, neither the prison nor the outside world (Wilson, 2000). Wilson talked of the in-between literacies of prisons as offering prisoners a space in which to compose. If this theoretical space is given to children's meaning-making what would it look like? By giving space to children's out-of-school literacies, many elements can come in. Third space can look like Figure 3.5.

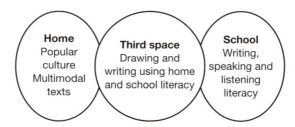

Figure 3.5 Third Space

Third space theory allows us to think about how children's meaning-making often lies between school and home. Children compose and write in after-school clubs, or with friends, and when they compose at home they are drawing on school stuff and when they compose at school they are using their home experience and practices. We revisit third space throughout this book as it is an important concept within New Literacy Studies. It provides us with an understanding of literacy which is linked to spaces, and provides a more *embodied* understanding of literacy.

ACTIVITY

Making a third space

Construct a 'third space' where your students can connect up out-of-school with their school literacies. Imagine the **artefacts**, **stories** and **resources** your students will develop. You can describe an activity, or devise a lesson drawing on home experiences. A metaphor for the home–school space where the two meet is of **wet sand**. A wave washes the sand, and makes it wet then retreats. The wet sand is the space between home and school, where children can create meanings across sites.

CHILDREN'S LITERACY AND POPULAR CULTURE

New thinking on literacy practices, and how texts and practices can be recontextualized across sites, has led to a way of thinking about children's literacy practices which acknowledges that they are hybrid and diverse. They can also take on meanings from children's popular culture. Console games and other television narratives can be drawn upon to create new 'mixed' meanings. In her work on African-American children's literacy, Dyson describes this process as 'remix' (Dyson, 2003). Likewise, in her work on digitized literacies, Marsh has argued for a revaluing of the textual meanings provided by children's popular culture, arguing that they offer a rich seam of meanings from which children can draw, write and orally retell stories (Marsh, 2003). Console games can become sources of narrative, often drawing on a number of different 'levels' in which to make new forms of meaning, layered and dependent on an understanding of how the games work. For example, a child drew the 'Spiderman' game as part of a writing journal, then covered it up to indicate that he had gone up a level (Graham, 2004).

Vignette: Children's response to console games

I watched Fatih draw a bird alongside a picture of Super Mario, a character from a console game. One evening, I visited Fatih's home. Fatih immediately began telling me about the Super Mario game he was playing, about the stages, the castle, the bricks, what he does. He was very excited. Fatih produced some drawings, which he proceeded to describe to me. Figure 3.6 shows a man pursued by a round two-legged thing, with a bird beneath it. Fatih described the drawing to me, 'That's Mario and that's the bird. That's sonic and that's the bomb, the bomb's chasing him he hasn't got no head'. Fatih's drawing reflected two strands of his life: his interest in Super Mario, and his Turkish identity as 'bird' or 'Kus'. When developing activities for him in the classroom, both identities come into play.

Figure 3.6 Image of bird and Super Mario

In her work on teachers and children's popular culture, Marsh argues that teachers are fearful of challenging the status quo by drawing on children's popular culture to develop literacy activities (Marsh, 2003). Yet, here Fatih, is representing meaning and taking from different cultural traditions in one drawing. By allowing both cultural influences to co-exist in one drawing, Fatih's different identities were expressed.

ACTIVITY

Picture worth a thousand words

Consider an image, picture or set of images, which you respond to strongly. This could be a well-known piece of art, or an advertisement or a postcard you like. Think about what you re-create in your head when you look at the image. What stories accompany the image?

Children's identities can often be expressed through their text-making. These identities shift in relation to the different ways children feel about the subject of their drawing and writing. As you saw in Chapter 2, Kress used the word 'interest' for the way in which children's interest in a text leads to meaning. He also invoked the word 'motivated' to describe how children decide to create certain ways of expressing meaning (Kress, 1997). Kress suggests that we call texts 'signs'. From this, he leads to the idea of the **motivated sign** that is created from children's interest at the time. At home, children make signs using all kinds of stuff: tissue paper, kitchen roll, cardboard and other miscellaneous bits of stuff which can be found around the home. Kress noticed that children made signs regularly and freely at home, using these texts in their play. Home, he suggests, can be a place where children make meaning using a variety of different kinds of stuff.

In studies of children's meaning-making at home, families from a wide range of socio-economic backgrounds supported children's meaning-making at home (see in particular, Pahl, 2002, and Marsh and Thompson, 2001). These children were able to draw on long-term narratives when making texts. Children drew on the different artefacts found in the home such as small toys and mini worlds. Different timescales were associated with different objects to be found at home.

Children's texts describe different cultural worlds. Kenner's (2000) work details the different worlds a child inhabits. These worlds may include community contexts such as mosque school, home contexts such as particular traditions within the home, cultural influences from satellite television, and neighbourhood influences.

Children's cultural worlds

Think of the different spaces children inhabit. Create a list of all the ways that popular culture can inhabit children's worlds. Lunch boxes, duvet covers, pyjamas can all bear logos from children's cultural worlds. The worlds could also include artefacts and objects children engage in when they play.

Figure 3.7 is an example, from Marsh (2003).

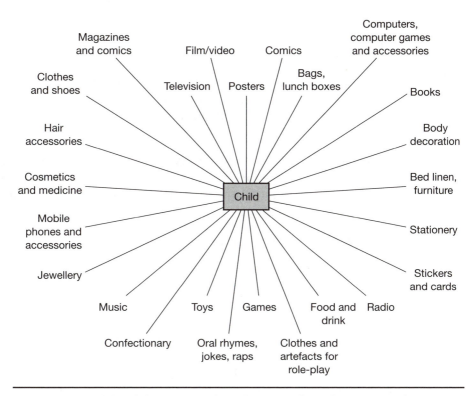

Figure 3.7 Children's Popular Cultural Worlds (Marsh, 2003: 114)

When linking up home and school the variety of children's popular cultural worlds needs to be considered. An 'asset' model can be applied, which acknowledges these influences as assets in the development of children's meaning-making. When children's texts go to school they can be readily comprehended and supported.

Yrjö Engeström on artefacts in activity systems

In Engeström's work in the area of activity theory, he argues that a thing in the environment can only become the object of an activity when it is mediated by actors – thereby investing meaning and motivating power in the object. Objects are cultural and collective constructs. Activity theory helps us to understand instances of practice and how artefacts like a bead map of Turkey made by a Turkish child with his mother's prayer beads provide important implications for how our students make meaning (Engeström, 1999).

CONCLUSION

This chapter has looked at a range of approaches to the development of children's literacy at school. It has considered the ways in which different programmes have supported children's literacy, and the different cultural worlds of children.

This chapter offers some directions for educators. It suggests that, 'educators learn to incorporate students' texts written outside school, but to understand and build on their literacy practices' (Schultz, 2002: 386). This perspective gives educators the challenge of:

- finding out about the literacy practices of their students;
- sharing them in a community of practice with the class;
- building on these practices in classroom settings.

Classrooms of the future may incorporate the ways in which homes work. Children at home draw on cultural identities, such as Fatih's 'Kus', plus their play, such as Fatih's console games, to develop their stories and composing. These different cultural experiences are often placed side by side. At home, movement across sites and across modes may be happening much more quickly and to a different time frame than at school. We need to examine what literacy activities our students are engaging with out of school and consider how we can form bridges to support students within school. This will give us the opportunity to think more clearly about what literacy is being supported where.

In addition, we need to pay attention to the complex blend of new and old media, which are central to the experience of the everyday cultures of childhood and adolescence (Carrington and Luke 2003). Like it or not, textual practices such as email, online shopping, webcams, messaging and games using avatars online are part of young people's realities. *It is time to take these forms into our schools and use them.*

CHAPTER 4

Bridging Local and Global Literacies

Vignette: Bringing school into the home and home into the school

In My-Linh Hang's reception class she creates digital student portfolios using digital pictures of students throughout the year (for example, activities, learning moments, field trips, and so on). These pictures are shared with both students and parents, most of whom are of EAL backgrounds, to communicate student learning and growth on an ongoing basis. My-Linh believes that despite language barriers, students and especially their parents appreciate and value seeing these pictures – 'it brought the school into the home and invited the home into the school'. My-Linh put up new bulletin board displays bi-weekly and students would narrate what they were doing and either attempt to write down their words using invented spelling or dictated their words to her to be scribed. As a result, she was not simply 'putting up pretty pictures of cute kids'. but there was an actual concrete purpose for writing and this manifests the school's communication between home and school. What is more, she would use the pictures to make the class read books aloud ('again the words would come from the students') and to make school 'home' movies using the software program I-movie to be viewed as a group during open houses, parent interviews or class celebrations.

KEY THEMES IN THE CHAPTER

- ■ *Research on local and global theory*
- ■ *Building on language variety in the classroom*
- ■ *Multiple literacies*
- ■ *Global identities*
- ■ *Working within global cultures*

INTRODUCTION

Imagine that you are working in a year 5 classroom with a mix of students from different cultures, with varying language needs, from lower and middle-class backgrounds, who practise different religions and belief systems. You work in a multicultural, urban school with families from a variety of cultures that make up the school's community. You are planning a language/history lesson on citizenship. You ask your students to write poems about their sense of belonging within their immediate culture. Then you teach them how to create a watermark on the computer, using a picture of themselves that the teacher takes with a digital camera. Students then create a poem about their sense of belonging, or lack of belonging, in their school and community, and they type their poem on the classroom computer and superimpose the text onto the student's photo. The message is a celebration of their old culture within a new one – the medium is a digital photo of them that can appear on screen or be printed.

In this chapter, the focus will be on the way global influences – the Internet, media, economic migration – are embedded within local contexts. Meaning can be gathered and held in the form of ways of speaking and telling stories, and taken across diasporas. How can language teaching reflect the globalized world we live in? Like previous chapters, this chapter bridges theory and research to offer ways of creating a language and literacy curriculum that builds on what children bring to literacy. Children bring themselves to the texts they read and make and their identities inform the meaning-making process. Children's linguistic, cultural, and socio-economic backgrounds play out in their literacy learning. When they engage in new contexts, they bring local and global funds of knowledge to those contexts.

The chapter considers how to relate local/global concerns to classroom practice. How does the New Literacy Studies help us to teach in classrooms where children bring their many languages to literacy learning? This chapter builds on Chapter 3 with its emphasis on family literacies informing school literacy teaching; the crossing of sites is an important area of inquiry and thought for literacy teachers.

Local classroom contexts are tied to global contexts. Just as literacy events and practices are bound to classroom contexts, to teachers and to students so, too, local-based practices and assumptions are bound to larger, global practices and assumptions. By situating literacy within the local and the global, issues such as 'global economies' and 'global markets' become important and relevant to our learning and our understanding of language. Global economies and global markets are tied to classroom language teaching in that the New Literacy Studies are most concerned with embodied understandings of meaning and of knowledge.

ACTIVITY

Children's embodied understandings

Take a piece of text from any genre. Ask yourself these questions:

> Why was this text written?
> Who wrote it?
> What do you bring to the text (as a person; as a teacher; as a text-maker)?
> What kind of language is used in the text?
> Is it specific or general?
> Which bits of the text are tied to local contexts?
> Which bits of the text are tied to global contexts?

The activity illustrates our taken-for-granted understanding of reading and writing processes. Young children possess a similar understanding that grows with time and with our fluency of different ways of speaking. Such an activity facilitates a meta-awareness of the **embodied** nature of reading and writing specifically, but as well of how we exist in what Etienne Wenger calls 'communities of practice' (Wenger, 1998).

Think back to Fatih's bird in Chapter 3, which he constructed using Super Mario characters (although a bird does not exist in the Super Mario game). We discussed the importance of birds within Fatih's cultural framework or lived experience – the complex interweaving of different parts of himself within the learning process. Fatih's embodied understandings led him to transfer or transform one cultural/embodied understanding to another – Super Mario. This is as much a learning context as studying gears and pulleys as part of a science unit. Literacy teachers today have to move beyond such practical issues as decoding print to take equal account of the ideas beneath writing.

These ideas could be accounting for:

- the social, cultural and economic ideas embedded in the content of texts;

- the intended audience of a text;

- the function of a text;

- whether a text is print or electronic and why one over the other;

- whether the text was produced locally or globally.

To illustrate what 'literacy in its social context' means, let us return to the vignette at the beginning of the chapter. My-Linh teaches in an urban reception classroom. She has as multicultural a classroom as you can imagine, with students from mostly lower socio-economic backgrounds. A governing philosophy in My-Linh's classroom is to create an inclusive classroom by creating a community within her classroom. She does so not by blurring her students' cultural identities or introducing an entirely new identity for them to adopt, but instead by having them slowly find their place within the community.

In My-Linh's classroom she teaches children with experience of migration – of multiculturalism – and of global and economic integration which intensifies as the gap between local worlds and global worlds lessens. You feel it in your teaching when you work with a group of students from different cultures and families and you discuss new media they use or a website they visit. When cultures and linguistic diversity collide they transform into a new experience for everyone and incite a new community of practice for everyone involved.

Etienne Wenger: Communities of practice

Etienne Wenger argues that we belong to **communities of practice** – at home, at school, at work, in our hobbies – we belong to several different communities of practice at once. They are so informal and so pervasive that they rarely come into explicit focus, but for the same reasons they are also quite familiar. As individuals, learning is an issue of engaging in and contributing to the practices of our communities. For communities, this entails refining practices and ensuring new generations of members. Learning is an integral part of our everyday lives and learning generally takes place within communities. Communities of practice are created over time by the sustained pursuit of a shared experience (Wenger, 1998).

This form of inquiry looks beyond the practical in our language teaching to understand what ideas lie beneath our texts, our practices, our understandings and our assumptions. How we make meaning is tied to where and within what set of values, forms of knowledge and underlying meanings we read and we write. The New Literacy Studies looks at *literacy as a social practice*. In doing so, the theories then take account of the local and of the global. **Global literacies** mean that we need to take account of our students' cultural identities. This puts the focus back onto meaning, the ways in which some students carry their narratives of migration with them across contexts, into new settings and new cultural identities.

Allan and Carmen Luke: Local–global flows of knowledge

Communities of practice rely on a variety of factors tied to larger influences. In their writings, Allan and Carmen Luke discuss the interdependent relationship between the local and the global within such forces as flows of knowledge. By 'flows of knowledge' they mean: how knowledge makes its way into different communities from one context to the next; issues of power and who controls capital within local contexts and across local and global contexts; and the way local contexts reinterpret global events. In this way, the local–global continuum cuts across all levels of society and culture *and* literacy; through traditional and new communicational systems like the Web we have new vehicles for articulating this relationship (Luke and Luke, 2000).

GLOBAL LITERACY AS MULTIMODAL

As noted in earlier chapters, meaning is made in ways that are increasingly multimodal whereby written, that is, linguistic modes of meaning work in synchronization with the visual, the audio and spatial patterns of meaning. Take, for example, rock videos with their fusillade of music, of dance, of gesture and of visual animation, to create a certain mood with a particular message. Most of our communicational systems rely on multimodality to create a message.

Given that the substance, content and aesthetics of multimodality rely on the global and globalization, we should account for multimodality in our meaning-making. It follows that if we should understand the relationship between multimodality and globalization, we equally should understand how the multimodal and the global function within local contexts.

> **ACTIVITY**
>
> ### Isolating the local in the global and the global in the local
>
> To develop a sense of the local in the global, collect two newspaper articles: one on a local event and one on an international event. Ideally, find the local article in an international newspaper and an international article in a local paper. Discuss perspective in both articles (authorial voice, use of language, different Discourses, photographs, format and layout) and the relationship between the local and the global.
>
> Ask yourself these questions:
>
> How does the content differ?
> Is there a significant difference between the layout and overall visual communication of the two texts?
> How has the author situated herself or himself in the article?

LOCAL AND GLOBAL LITERACIES IN THE CLASSROOM

In urban classrooms, where there are students from a variety of cultures, such as Turkish, Afro-Caribbean and Serbo-Croatian students, there are ways of respecting cultural practices within the curriculum, through a multimodal approach, like in drama, in role-play, in music, in computers and through the arts. For example, a tile project took place in a Turkish community in a school in North London, which encouraged children to work on their drawings of plants in science and turn them into Turkish tiles – linking science and the arts.

A global approach to literacy implies an understanding of the power relations around literacy. Globalization has and does supply a context for different kinds of research on literacy. An example of different kinds of research is to look at language. How we speak in one local context can be quite different from a neighbouring local context. Comparing and contrasting language use in the two contexts helps us to understand complex sets values, beliefs and agendas. Language – how and when it is used – separates one society from the next. Such theorizing led to a belief in the situated nature of language. Language practices can change to meet local conditions.

> ### *Vignette: Infusing global literacies in your classroom*
>
> *Sue Pedersen designs her classroom with illustrations and photographs from different cultures. She has a separate reading area with soft cushions with a rich library filled with dual-language texts, wordless picture books, non-fiction texts, comic books, Pokémon cards and stories of all sorts from fables to Harry Potter. It is a classroom that celebrates different cultures and appeals strongly to the interests of students in the class. Sue has a 'publishing centre' in the middle of her classroom where children laminate, collate and bind books of their poetry, drawings and stories in English and, at times, in their own language. These books are on display around the room and in a central area of the school.*
>
> *Sue has a specific philosophy of literacy that embraces all forms of literacy and invites linguistic diversity. Sue does not insist that students adopt one culture and one language, but instead allows and encourages them to adapt their own culture and language to their host language and culture. In this way, one language begets another.*

If we are to understand the relationship between power relations and literacy, we need to understand how the cultural background of our students relates to classroom practice. The vignettes above and at the beginning of the chapter illustrate how we can harness our language teaching to culture and cultural practice by incorporating and building on students' lived experiences in our teaching.

When we scaffold our students' home culture and social practices within their schooling contexts, students are able to situate themselves in the process. They can find themselves in the local and in the global and embed their identities in artefacts like a poem on a digital image. That is, they can bring a part of themselves tied to family and their birthplace and re-create it in a contemporary medium. After all, children are the masters of our new communicational systems and by combining them with more traditional methods we are speaking to their needs and to their interests.

Teaching to global literacies

What to think about when you are teaching students literacy:

- The way we question students about language (that is, how our assumptions inform their assumptions).
- The types of texts we use (combine print with electronic, mix genres, offer exposure to home texts and school texts).

▶

- Interview students about the texts they read at home and with their friends.
- Account for multimodality (Kress, 1997) in meaning-making.
- Have students think about how their everyday practices relate to global events/influences.
- Embed an understanding of Discourses (Gee, 1996) and practices in language use.
- What is the function of the texts students use?
- Account for how language has changed and how we can see this in texts.
- Encourage students to use different modes.

LOCAL LITERACIES IN GLOBAL LITERACIES

Deborah Brandt and Katie Clinton explore in their article, 'The limits of the local', the evolution of the New Literacy Studies, discussing studies that led to literacy as a social practice as a framework (Brandt and Clinton, 2002). Formerly, many literacy theorists and educators adopted a *cognitive* model of literacy development whereby we carry language skills with us and it is through teaching and usage that we become literate. In the work of Brandt and Clinton, they maintain that *social context* organizes literacy as opposed to literacy organizing social context.

In an *autonomous model of literacy*, as discussed in Chapter 1, texts dictate terms for the reader, whereas in an *ideological model of literacy*, the reader and the context dictate the terms of how a text is read and understood. Such a shift in thinking gives more power to the reader and the context as carriers of their own meanings, discourses and ideologies. All of this we understand as being part of the theories described within the New Literacy Studies. What has not been accounted for as much is the relationship between local practices and their tie to globalization. Just as Discourses exist within discourses, so too Cultures (to take up Gee's use of upper and lower cases) exist within cultures. If we locate the way we embed our culture and our history into our literacy teaching and learning, and equally the way students embed their culture and history into their literacy learning, we are that much closer to understanding where our literacy skills and assumptions end and where global influences begin.

Brandt and Clinton: The local and the global

Deborah Brandt and Katie Clinton argue that detailed ethnographic studies, which demonstrate the role of identity and context in language development, need to be located within a larger, global framework. If we regard *literacy as a global and social practice*, we have to analyse how we communicate across cultures within a global space. Brandt and Clinton draw from the work of Bruno Latour in arguing for a local–global continuum within a literacy framework. Latour speaks of an Ariadne's thread that allows us to pass seamlessly from the local to the global (Brandt and Clinton, 2002).

The local and the global rely on each other and manifest themselves in our artefacts, in our speech and in our practices. There is an increasing nexus between what goes on locally and what goes on globally. There is a thread of networks and practices that cuts across cultures, sites, communities of practice and identities in practice from textbooks used in South Africa by global publishing corporations like Thomson Publishing to standardized tests administered in Asia, the USA and so on.

We see the local and the global in all manner of websites used in locations such as Cardiff, Wales, and in Edmonton, Alberta. All is made of local interactions. Every text and practice bear traces of former texts and practices. However, studying literacy from strictly inside the frame (that is, strictly from a local perspective), global contexts get lost or blurred. According to Brandt and Clinton, the process of obfuscating the global has a tendency for some researchers to concentrate overly on the local without foregrounding traces of global influences.

Forms of literacy that bridge local and global

There are certain literacies which are simultaneously local and global. That is, they take place in local settings but rely on global networks. These are:

1   literacy for establishing and maintaining relationships (for example, email, texting);
2   literacy for accessing or displaying information (for example, PowerPoint, Internet searches, SGML or XML coding);
3   literacy for pleasure and/or self-expression (for example, web pages, videogames);
4   literacy for skills development (for example, combining media in written assignments).

ADOPTING A MULTILITERACIES FRAMEWORK

When we return to New Literacy Studies teachers presented in the book so far – such as Angie, Anne and Andras – it is clear that theory and research in this area leads us to a teaching framework that builds on theory and practice in the past. In their work, the New London Group who devised a pedagogy of multiliteracies have offered a pedagogy that meets the communicational and cultural needs of contemporary students.

Jo Lo Bianco, in 'Multiliteracies and multilingualism', described how the effect of English assuming the function of 'lingua mundi' means that, 'a complex dynamic of cultural politics emerges' (Bianco, 2000: 93). Bianco describes how language change needs to be understood in the context of globalization, 'with its hybrid language and cultural forms' (Bianco, 2000: 94). Globalization has brought with it a plethora of other Discourses and cultural forms, and our students have the most savvy with it.

Bianco described examples of language and literacy practices that offer a challenge to traditional curricula because of their complexity. He draws on Saxena's account of Panjabi families in Southall, and describes the complexity of the three different scripts which Panjabi families employ in their life:

- Panjabi written in Gurmukkhi scripts associated with Sikhs;

- Hindi written in Devanagari script and associated with Hindus;

- Urdu which is written in Perso-Arabic script and associated with Muslims (Saxena, 2000).

This pattern of **multilingual** scripts being associated with different practices is one which is familiar to multilingual households, who may carry a number of different oral and written linguistic practices within them. In many countries, such as India, a household will draw on local words for the days of the week or the months of the year, as well as nationally recognized words. An English speaker speaking Hindi in a global setting would use English words, inserted into Hindi. In doing so, the local–global flow of knowledge, as Luke and Luke express it, is realized (Luke and Luke, 2000). Return to My-Linh's class with Urdu students and students from Angola and we appreciate how classrooms need to be set up differently so that everyone finds a place.

A pedagogy of multiliteracies: the New London Group

1 **Situated practice**: a student's immersion into meaningful practices within a community of learners who are capable of playing multiple and different roles based on their backgrounds and experience. Situated practice must consider the socio-cultural needs and identities of all learners.

2 **Overt instruction**: a teacher's intervention into the meaning-making process by scaffolding learning activities. Students gain explicit information to organize and guide their learning. The goal of overt instruction is to develop a student's conscious awareness and control over what is being learned.

3 **Critical framing**: a student frames his or her teaching and learning around such embodied understandings as culture, politics, ideologies, values and beliefs. Teachers thereby denaturalize and 'make strange' what they have been taught and learned. Through critical framing, students can constructively critique what they have learned and account for its cultural, political and socio-economic implications.

4 **Transformed practice**: a teacher can develop new ways in which students can demonstrate how they can design and carry out new practices embedded in their goals and values. Transformed practice allows students to apply and revise what they have learned — and do so critically and, as a result, more meaningfully (Cope and Kalantzis, 2000: 35).

MULTILITERACIES FRAMEWORK: SITUATED PRACTICE

In this section, we focus on the role of teaching and pedagogy in constructing local and global spaces for learning. As the first of four components to the multiliteracies framework conceived by Cope and Kalantzis and the group of scholars that gathered to forge a new language pedagogy, situated practice works from a base of students' own interests and life-world experience (Cope and Kalantzis, 2000: 240). Grounded on real-life experience, students use their prior knowledge, from home, from school, from communities and from culture, to contribute to their language learning.

Nancy Hornberger: The continua of biliteracy

Research in multilingual settings contributes to a situated practice approach to language teaching. Nancy Hornberger analyses a concept she calls 'the continua of biliteracy'. Hornberger uses the term 'biliteracy' to signal that communication takes place in two or more languages and in classrooms around the world, this is taking place (Hornberger, 2000). In most urban classroom settings, students bring a mosaic of cultures and languages. Teachers commonly draw on their students' different languages in this kind of setting. For example, teachers may use their students' home languages to get a point across or use dual-language texts when creating displays. Hornberger's work suggests that learning contexts should allow learners to draw from their different language backgrounds and, in doing so, language teachers are providing greater chances for switching between, or even among, languages for greater expression. As a result, students are able to use all of the linguistic resources they have to hand (Hornberger, 2000).

Like Hornberger, researcher Larry Condelli maintains that when teachers in his study used native languages as part of instruction to clarify and explain points, students showed faster growth in both reading comprehension and oral communication skills. Condelli carried out a comprehensive survey of how literacy was being taught to EAL learners, and devised recommendations from the research. By using learners' native languages in the classroom, learning is achieved more quickly. According to Condelli, since the directions for a language and literacy task are often more complex than the language required to complete the task itself, students who received clarification in their first language were able to focus on the task at hand (Condelli, 2003). For instance, if you have to assemble a piece of furniture or cook something, directions can be in another language and the student simply needs to follow illustrations.

One of the key findings of his study is connecting literacy teaching to everyday life. To implement Condelli's strategy, teachers used materials from daily life which contained information that students wanted to know about, or with which they had some experience. Victoria Purcell-Gates et al. also argue that using objects from everyday experiences encourages students to embed their lived experience into their language learning (Purcell-Gates et al., 2002). Cultural practices and views of the world that students bring to class can and should be used in teaching language and literacy to students. In this way, not only are practices taken across sites, but literacy practices in classrooms are imbued with the cultural meanings and lived experience of out-of-school literacies and linguistic repertoires.

Vignette: Charting cultural migrations

In Andras Valezy's year 8 intermediate/advanced English as a Second Language class, students worked on a biography unit that tied together concepts of the local and the global. As part of the project, students were expected to invoke a variety of designs in the context of a multimodal approach to language. They relied on this approach to develop their ideas into short published works.

Students began by reading a biography of Terry Fox with their teacher. After finishing the story they proceeded to identify the distinguishing features of biographical writing. Students were asked to work in groups in order to formulate questions that biographers might ask their subjects. They were also encouraged to pick an older family member who had immigrated to Canada. Andras then asked them to think of some relevant questions that could be used in an interview if they were to write a narrative of this person's life.

To facilitate subject-related discussions students were asked to bring photos of the chosen family member to class. Most of the students brought pictures that chronicled a story of migration from their country of origin to Canada. The photos were an excellent catalyst for generating discussion in class. Students expressed interest in each other's photos and enthusiastically shared stories about their parents or grandparents.

Using the questions they had generated previously, students went home and interviewed their family. Many of the biographies focused on how these individuals' lives differed as they grew up in other parts of the world from their new lives in Canada; furthermore, the students' work explored issues and various factors that motivated their chosen subject to immigrate to Canada.

The remainder of the project was completed in the information technology (IT) room. With the aid of word-processing programs (Appleworks and Word), students used their notes from the interviews to author biographies. Andras then helped them to scan their photos in order to incorporate them into their stories. Along with these pictures students used Internet resources to import maps, flags and other relevant images that served to complement the written text. They also designed a cover page and wrote captions under the imported images. The project generated student input on a variety of topics, including differences in social conditions and culture as well as the economic disparities that exist between various countries. Students finished their work by publishing the stories, but the greatest satisfaction they got from the completion of their assignment was the opportunity to share it with their families.

By welcoming the linguistic resources students bring to class, language learners are placed within contexts that acknowledge what they have to offer within a classroom setting. Multiple literacies involve several different language varieties and scripts, complex and multiple repertoires which can be documented through ethnographic observation. That is, these same linguistic differences and visual and oral repertoires are carried over into different communicative events. For example, when we move from a schooling setting to a commercial setting like a department store, we are still using language varieties and scripts, and the same can be said when we travel across settings. In many everyday contexts, dual languages are common. For example, in Wales, train announcements and notices are commonly presented in Welsh and English.

ACTIVITY

Accounting for communicative repertoires

Contexts therefore carry what Hornberger terms 'communicative repertoires' or sets of communicative practices (for example, talking, describing, listening, gesturing, and so on). Classroom contexts have students with different communicative repertoires. Think of a bilingual student you have taught or who is in your class at the moment. List some of the communicative repertoires required of the student, for example:

Mosque: Arabic
Classroom: English
Home: Turkish

Consider how the contexts in which the repertoire is used changes the way language is viewed or used (Hornberger, 2000).

Children acquire home languages at different rates, and acquire different language systems using different ways of instruction. Eve Gregory has documented how Bangladeshi children learn Arabic using very different pedagogical models to the way they acquire or develop their English in schools (Gregory, 1997).

MULTILITERACIES FRAMEWORK: OVERT INSTRUCTION

Overt instruction involves comparing and contrasting different kinds of conventions of meaning in different cultural contexts: the social context of your school's community; the professional Discourse (Gee, 1996) of teaching and curriculum; your students' cultural capital (Cope and Kalantzis, 2000: 240). Overt instruction peels back the layers of ideas and concepts you teach to uncover underlying systems and structures; how meaning is organized, by whom and when.

In our speaking, in our listening, and in our actions, there is a mixing and melding together of different voices, which form a mix of our communicative repertoires. Theorists in the area of New Literacy Studies speak of **hybridity** in this light: as a blending of linguistic repertoires and accompanying practices within situated speech.

Dinah Volk: Syncretic literacies

Researchers like Dinah Volk found that children blend literacy practices. These literacy practices come from:

- home;
- school;
- popular culture;
- religion;
- community groups (Volk, 1997).

She described the complex web of continuities and discontinuities in language-use patterns of 5-year-olds. Volk argued that parents speaking to their children at home insert patterns of interaction from school into home practices.

Blending cultural patterns across diasporas was the focus of Duranti and Ochs research on literacy practices of the Samoan community in the USA. They observed families' literacy practices at home. They blended existing practices taken from Samoa, involving family artefacts, with schooled literacy practices when supporting their children with reading. They used the term *syncretic*, to describe the blending of different practices, from different sources and cultures (Duranti and Ochs, 1996).

In everyday life, we mix popular cultural texts with long-standing community and social practices and traditions. There is a rich vein of inquiry and relevance to language teaching when we account for complex mixes of cultural traditions within our speech patterns. Appreciating the local and the global and the local cultural identity of our students opens up opportunities for richer classroom experiences. Many researchers have located the intersection of culture and new media and its impact on language. Hornberger identifies the concept of 'sites' and 'worlds' where linguistic repertoires are used, which could be, for example, home and school, or mosque and school.

Ben Rampton: Code-switching

Ben Rampton in his analysis of urban youth's linguistic practices used the term *code-switching* to describe how urban young men use a number of different linguistic resources in different settings, switching from, for example, Black patois, 'Bangla' to white slang (Rampton, 1992). The term code-switching was first used by Gumperz when describing different interactive practices and how communicators shift from one linguistic code to another (Gumperz, 1982).

ACTIVITY

Charting code-switching

Reflect on the different linguistic worlds or speech communities in which you function. These could be:

   as a teacher;
   as a parent;
   as a writer;
   as someone involved in politics;
   as a member of a local community;
   as a reader.

Write them down.

   Take note of your speech in different contexts and describe how you code-switch. Note these points down:

   Are there any patterns in your own code-switching?
   Did you notice your students code-switching?
   Did you notice anyone else code-switching (for example, administrators, friend, and so on).
   What does the interaction of different codes tell you about language teaching?

MULTILITERACIES FRAMEWORK: CRITICAL FRAMING

Critical framing extends overt instruction by reflecting on embodied understandings in texts of all kinds (Figure 4.1). As Cope and Kalantzis express it, critical framing interrogates contexts and purposes, adding breadth to our perspective on our identities and social contexts. Typically, when adopting critical framing in your teaching you would be asking, why do texts work in this way? It is an interpretation of the social and cultural contexts of meaning (Cope and Kalantzis, 2000: 247).

Figure 4.1 Students working with and critically framing new technologies

Jim Cummins: Negotiating identities in multilingual classrooms

In Jim Cummins's work, he reflects on identity negotiation within classroom contexts – particularly multicultural classroom contexts. Cummins looks at micro interactions between students and teachers as image-forming. In his research he shows how the current push in literacy for standardized tests and increasing endorsement of traditional or, as he expresses it, 'scripted' literacy instruction through phonological interventions prevent students' negotiation of identity in classrooms. Cummins claims that empowerment for students results from a collaborative creation of power. In the classroom, a collaborative creation of power relies on interaction between teacher and student. Based on Cummins's research, power is created and shared within this interpersonal space where minds and identities meet. Cummins speaks of a 'triangular set of images':

1 an image of our own identities as educators;

2 an image of the identity options we highlight for our students;

3 an image of the society we hope our students will help form.

Cummins argued that notions of identity or power negotiation in teaching and learning do not appear in policy documents or in 'positivistic scientific research', but they do very much appear in many of the qualitative ethnographies conducted by researchers such as Moll et al., 1992 (Cummins, 2001).

ACTIVITY

Negotiating identities in the classroom

Draw a Venn diagram (Figure 4.2, two intersecting circles with a common space). In one circle, write the word 'Identity' and write down words and thoughts you have on the role of identity in the classroom. In the other circle, write the word 'Community' and write down words and thoughts you have about working as a community in the classroom. In the common area, write down words and thoughts that bring the two concepts together. Reflect on when and how the two concepts converge or intersect.

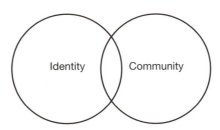

Figure 4.2 Community and identity

Vignette: Getting to know someone

Steve Pirso, a year 4 teacher, and Marianna Diiorio, a teacher-librarian, worked collaboratively with Steve's students to create a multimedia project on poetry. To begin with, the students were immersed in a variety of poems. Their teachers read and dramatized poems, and talked about various characteristics of the different forms of poetry. Students were then divided into two smaller groups, one using computers to learn the software needed for the project and the other focused on choral readings of poems for two voices. The choral readings were taped using a digital video camera and then edited using I-movie. Students also wrote poems and used a word-processing program to publish their poems. They used colour and pencil crayons to illustrate their poems. The illustrations were scanned and saved using the school's server. As a cumulative activity, the class collaboratively wrote a poem entitled 'We know someone' based on a poem in Michael Rosen's My Song is Beautiful entitled, 'I Know Someone'. The students performed this work, which was also taped and edited using I-movie. Finally, all the pieces were pulled together using I-movie. The project resulted in a multimedia video that included video clips, voice-overs, back-ground music, titles and transitions.

Once completed, the students had an opportunity to share their work with their families. Students were able to borrow a CD copy or a video copy of the work. This enterprise gave families a chance to see the diversity of students in Steve's class and to recognize how hard they work together.

MULTILITERACIES FRAMEWORK: TRANSFORMED PRACTICE

The end result of situating practice, overtly instructing, and critically framing language teaching is *transformed practice*. According to Cope and Kalantzis, this is making transferred meanings and putting them to work in other contexts or cultural sites. Transformed practice teaches students to have meta-awareness of their embodied understandings and to guide them to inform their understandings, their reading and their writing (that is, their meaning-making). Transformed practice enables students to bring their embodied understandings into other contexts and cultural sites (Cope and Kalantzis, 2000: 35).

Transformed practice can help us teach specific language skills that are contemporary and far more differentiated than a stable, sound-letter correspondence approach which has been the traditional approach to literacy teaching and learning. Gone are the days of decoding phonemes to learn to read and make texts. To effectively teach today's students we should take equal account of:

1 their communicative repertoire;

2 their embodied understandings of language – in local and global perspectives.

For example, a number of different researchers have included semiotic systems in their approaches to multilingualism. Kenner, for example, documented how young children worked across sign systems and used a variety of different modes, including drawing and writing to express their meanings (Kenner, 2000). By recognizing that students who speak a number of languages move across a range of semiotic systems when they make meaning, a way of analysing the EAL classroom can be developed. When a child moves from a mathematics lesson on tessellations to a history lesson on explorers, they not only move across subject areas, but also across semiotic systems, across value systems and across embedded meanings and their assumptions (and implications). Language learners need to understand a wide range of discourse strategies which may go beyond grammar and pragmatics. Interaction is set in a wider social context, which needs to be analysed in order to focus on the needs of the learner. Recognizing the value of semiotic systems which engage in different community language contexts provides a more nuanced reading of how languages are used in twenty-first century contexts. For example, a child may draw on English to describe a football team, but may then write in Chinese script to compose a birthday card, switching to a Pokémon or Nike brand name to provide another dimension to the text.

THE HOME WITHIN THE SCHOOL

What lies at the heart of this chapter, is a focus on the home *within* the school. The home and the school are in **dialogic** relationship to each other. Each influences the other and speaks to the other, and these voices mix and merge. Children bring their culture and their cultural practices into primary classrooms and find their way into language and into print from a specific cultural lens which guides their literacy practices. It is clear from many of the powerful ethnographic studies presented in earlier chapters that fine-grained ethnographic studies of contexts such as the Piedmont Carolinas, Liberia, West Africa, Lancaster, UK, and Iran (Scribner and Cole, 1981; Heath, 1983; Street, 1984; Barton and Hamilton, 1998) elucidate the dialogic relationships between home cultures and schooling cultures, and these studies provide space to voice concerns about the way literacy is being taught and understood in our schools.

School literacy can dominate the home. One of our goals in writing this book is to encourage you, as literacy educators, to support the flow between meaning-making at home and meaning-making at school. There should not be a dissonant relationship between these contexts but a dialogic one, where multilingual language practices can be built on and fostered in the students' new culture and new schooling models. *Children are mediators of literacy.* We should structure activities and relationships in such a way that children can develop greater ownership over school-authorized literacy practices. Adopting a multiliteracies framework takes us that much closer to meeting the contemporary literacy needs of our students. Studies of out-of-school literacy practices should turn more of a focus on out-of-school *informing* in-school practices. These studies may describe practices, which may not initially make sense but will provide a richer understanding of our students' life worlds.

Vignette: Fatih's bead map

Fatih, a Turkish 5-year-old boy, was learning map-making at school. He drew maps of how to get to Granny's house from Red Riding Hood's house. He also was interested in flags, and in his family literacy class he made Turkish flags. As part of an ethnographic research project, Fatih's meaning-making was followed at home. Fatih was observed making an outline of a country, Turkey, with his mother's prayer beads on the kitchen table (see Figure 4.3). Fatih's mother was a devout Muslim and yet she allowed her son to make shapes of countries with her prayer beads. Fatih's uncle worked in Saudi Arabia and the family had migrated from Turkey to the UK. When I asked Fatih's mother, Elif, about the bead map shapes, she said,

Elif: *Do you know sometimes he … er … just er, for mine I explain …*

Kate: *Show me*
       (She gets some prayer beads and makes a shape).

E: *Lots of these making these …*

K: *Fatih makes?*

E: *No!*

K: *You make?*

E: *No … playing this.*

K: *Beads?*

E: *After the prayer he making. (laughs) He make it like this on the carpet.*

K: *Yeah?*

▶

> E: Like any,
>
> K: A shape?
>
> E: Which country.
>
> K: Ah I like that!
>
> E: I said Ireland he make it different like how Turkey like this. I said Turkey like this I said Turkey different very different I said England, Arabia I said, he make all! (laughs)
>
> Fatih then traced the outline of his country of origin on the kitchen table (see Figure 4.3)

Figure 4.3 Fatih's bead map

This vignette illustrates the power of the global in informing local practices. As Fatih traced the outlines of the countries, he was tracing the economic migration of his family across diasporas. He was exploring the global migratory patterns that led him to London, UK, in a multimodal form. This activity could have been carried over into the classroom, and his map-making, explored using traditional stories, could have been infused with global contexts.

CONCLUSION

How can these ideas be used in the classroom? Many practitioners working within a New Literacy Studies framework would argue that effective literacy learning in current educational climates can now occur only *outside* school settings. As practitioners, we should bring these theories into the classroom and use them in the following ways:

- as a framework for language teaching;
- to think about race and language;
- to incorporate multimodality into literacy teaching and learning;
- to diversify and blur gender lines;
- to account for forms and funds of knowledge in our planning and teaching.

By supporting our students, we recognize the value of their local/global knowledge, we are also valuing their literacy, and fostering their identities in practice and across diasporas.

REFLECTION

On the local and global in elementary teaching

This autumn I observed a recently converted Muslim student teach a year 2 class composed primarily of Muslim students. The topic of the lesson was celebration and naturally Chi-Binh and the students focused on Ramadan. What I found particularly interesting about the lesson was the cultural capital (Bourdieu, 1991) students had over Chi-Binh's more scholarly knowledge of the religion. From a theological context, Chi-Binh could discuss rituals and their purposes and significance, however, on cultural points children could fill out a picture of celebrating Ramadan with family and friends and differing perspectives on rituals. What struck me most sitting in an inner city school in Toronto was the fusion of old and new, of young and old, of crossing domains and sharing rituals, and perhaps more importantly, of local interpretations of a global faith. Chi-Binh learned a

▶

great deal from the cultural enrichment and expression of Islam and about being a Muslim offered by students in his class, and equally, students appreciated having a teacher who shared their faith and who possessed such an in-depth knowledge of their religion. Chi-Binh shared his feelings of working with the group of students during his practicum: 'I'm just remembering how excited the Muslim students of the class were about sharing what they knew, and I think that it did make a difference to them that I wasn't just someone who knew about Islam but that I was also someone who shared in their beliefs.'

CHAPTER 5

Literacy and Identity: Who Are the Meaning-makers?

Vignette: The role of identity in teaching

Several times a year I observe student teachers teach in classroom sites based on what they have learned in their teacher education programme. Whenever I observe teacher candidates teach, I learn something new about the nature of teaching and, what is more, I have a chance to see the personalities I teach demonstrate what they have learned about practice, pedagogy, policy, theory and, ultimately, about themselves as teachers. What strikes me most in my observations and discussions with them is how they embed parts of themselves in their teaching and, equally, how student learning is always and everywhere filtered through identities and everything students bring to the classroom. To illustrate, I present a morning at an urban primary school in which I was struck by the recurring role of identity on practical and ideological levels in teaching and learning.

Lisa McNeill: *extending a unit on radio drama with a year 5 group, Lisa asked the class to create costumes for characters in a radio drama based on descriptions of them in the text. Lisa presented her own interpretations, and asked the class to conjure up their own image of the person – their dress, their deportment, their sense of style. What amazed me as I walked around the room was the diverse, eclectic interpretations of characters. Each student had a very different sense of what a character would look and sound like if we were to meet them in class or on the street. Student identities were interwoven into their presentations and I remarked at how acute year 5 students' sense of style and manners of dress were.*

▶

Simon Ives: *Simon started a unit on feudal society in his year 4 classroom site by looking at the lifestyles of people during feudal times. Simon presented the very different rites and practices of people who lived during feudal times from the privileges of rulers to the wealth of landowners to the poverty of workers, to the regal nature of soldiers and knights. Simon asked students to imagine what it would be like to take on one of these identities and conjure a picture of the nature of their lives. In this way, students juxtaposed their own situation with those of feudal identities, contriving stories about what it would feel like to exist within different identities in such times.*

Robyn Cunningham: *for a visual arts lesson in her year 6 classroom, Robyn looked at the history of mosaics as expressions of beliefs at one time and, increasingly, as expressions of one's identity. She began the lesson with the lights off, but with the soft lighting of candles strewn around the room. She showed a series of mosaics from different times and asked students to think about what each one says about the age, about the artist and so on. After the slide show, students went to their desks and Robyn asked them to depict parts of themselves within a mosaic and they discussed their work with peers.*

By sheer chance, I walked into these three, consecutive teaching moments one morning with identity on my mind and what I faced as I moved from one classroom to the next, was identity at the heart and soul of each lesson. What strikes me time and time again is the degree to which this work of teaching the mediating of identities in teaching is developed within **micro** *(classroom) factors,* **meso** *(school administration level) and* **macro** *forces level. This teaching reflects the complex identities of our students.*

KEY THEMES IN THE CHAPTER

- *Identities in practice*
- *Identities in artefacts*
- *Discursive identity and literacy*
- *Multimodal identity and literacy*
- *Identity, teaching and learning*

INTRODUCTION

Imagine a classroom in which you do not think about identity on a daily – if not hourly – basis. Imagine a programme and a curriculum that does not account for multiple identities within a space? Would you want to teach in such a space?

This chapter looks at the most important ingredient in teaching and learning literacy, *identity*. The way we express our identity is partly through language. We also express our identity through our dress, artefacts we have around us, our accent, our way of talking, being and gesturing, and in our homes, communities and families. We create our identity through our *social practices*.

Language is used to construct an identity for ourselves within the different speech communities that we enter and we exit. When we speak we are thinking about *who* as in our audience, and *what* as in the content of our speech. What regulates both the *who* and the *what* is setting: in a classroom? At home with a parent? Sitting with friends? Talk relies on identities. Relationships are upheld through talk. We talk and act in one way at one moment and, equally, we are speaking and acting with someone at the same time and in the same moment. When we talk we reproduce our identity in practice. That is, our identity is supported in everyday social practice. One of the unspoken truths about teaching and learning is that the more agency we give to students, the more they learn.

In this chapter, we consider how identities are formed and form in the sites we inhabit, whether it is as a classroom teacher or as a year 4 student or as a parent working with a child at home. We consider the tool kits which we draw upon to represent identities. These tool kits can involve dress, talk, artefacts and other forms of representation. These tool kits can be used to invoke different identities.

In this chapter, we ask these questions:

- How do teachers infuse their classrooms with their own identities?

- How do students negotiate their identities in classrooms?

- How do parents' cultural identities infuse children's literacy practices?

When we consider identity, we also consider literacy. Literacy practices are infused with identity. Literacy is a culturally mediated and practice-infused activity that constantly pulls on the personality of the speaker, the writer or the reader. Our ways of being, speaking, writing and reading are intimately tied to our different discourse communities (as discussed in Chapters 1 and 4), which in turn shape our identities further. A discourse community can be a group of teenagers engaging in a chatroom, or a whole community sharing a common space, common terminology or language, and a common understanding of a set of practices (for example, working in a publishing company or working in a group as an adolescent learner in the classroom).

> ### Vignette: Displaying identity in halls and on walls
>
> *Val Petersen's classroom is in a multi-ethnic city in the North of England, and is aimed at young people who need support with literacy. The students are aged between 16 and 18. Her students are encouraged to express their identities through wall displays. A wall display called 'Young People Speak Out' gives students a sense that this space is where they are being heard. The display includes photographs of students, pictures of favourite rap artists, examples of student writing and images of the course and the classroom and activities taken using a digital camera. Students play music of their choice and surf the Net while engaging with literacy activities in the classroom. The students bookmark websites, and are in contact with their email or instant messaging as they work through the units of their online course. They also bring in their personal experience to discussions when they come together as a group. Their identities in practice are respected and heard.*

The chapter looks at how meaning-makers embed parts of themselves in their literacy practices and how identities are played out as they cross sites. What happens to Fatih's birds when he crosses sites from home to classroom? (See Chapter 3.) Why does a student's understanding of the genre of biography become more attuned when they write a biography of someone they know? (See Chapter 4.) Why does My-Linh take the time to take digital photographs of her students making-meaning in her classroom and why in turn do the parents so enjoy the process of seeing their children at work in her classroom at the end of the year? (Also see Chapter 4.)

Identity breathes life into literacy. People, both children and adults, have highly developed multilingual skills, for example, the ability to access websites in different languages. Students may draw on a number of different scripts, local and global languages. They might combine an interest in Bollywood musicals with a focus on their Indian heritage.

However, often, we do not have access to these things in school. Why is that? School often asks for students to remain within particular identities. A student may acquire a particular identity within a classroom, which may become fixed, for example, as being unable to read or write. Meanwhile, in Sunday school, the student is a competent writer. These two discursive identities are different. A discursive identity is one that is constructed within discourse, within speaking, and being in language. Why is it that so many adolescents, particularly boys, are labelled 'struggling readers' when they have advanced vocabularies and reading habits outside school in their use of popular media like Pokémon or Yu-Gi-Oh! game cards. Talk outside the school draws on different identities and competencies, including words like *Obelisk the Tormentor* or *Exodia* at home or with their peers, but in school they are silent. There is such a disparity between children's first worlds in their homes and communities and their second worlds with their peers, as compared to their schooling world. In Chapter 3, the expression *third space* was used to describe the meeting point between home and school, where the two worlds blend and mix. This third space can be filled with students' identities. Val's classroom, for example, offered students a third space where out-of-school literacies were allowed into the classroom. This was enabled through the use of the noticeboard where their words were put up with their photographs and posters of particular rap artists they liked. In this space, their identities were respected and heard.

SPACE AND IDENTITY

While school often may not provide a strongly supportive space for identity, there are other spaces. After-school clubs provide children with spaces to try out different identities in practice. Dance and gesture can be utilized to develop new identities. In an after-school club in London, a street-dancing class gave Black schoolchildren support for their out-of-school identities. Graffiti writing can be drawn upon in art projects and graffiti writing workshops can be used to engage street-wise teenagers.

A rap project in urban schools in Delaware (Meacham, 2004) gave students the opportunity to express thoughts and ideas through rap. Students who were feeling excluded from mainstream school were offered the opportunity to develop thoughts and ideas using the medium of rap. The group, Baseline Rappers, performed their words and produced a video of their work. They acquired literacy skills and confidence with performance and writing.

Hilary Janks and Barbara Comber are involved in an initiative in Australia and South Africa wherein students from a poor district of Johannesburg created alphabet books using words and images and artefacts from their community which they exchange with students in a similarly poor district of Adelaide. These books are expressions of their sense of identity within their space (Janks and Comber, 2004). These spaces are third spaces, neither home or classroom, where students' identities are upheld and transformed. Artefacts are used, such as posters, raps and websites, which are used as artefacts of identity, supporting and upholding students' identities. These link to the students' own cultural spaces, the **figured worlds** they create in order to develop and transform identities. (See theory box on Holland, 2001, below.)

Artefacts as traces of identity

Find an artefact at home or at school – one that you have made or that has been given to you or that you acquired – think about traces of yourself in the object (for example, a photograph of you and someone you love; a story that resonates with your own experience; an image that reminds you of a thought, a feeling, or an event that you have experienced). Describe what aspects of the artefact reflect your identity.

Our identities are formed bound up in the way in which we speak and we act. Writing and literacy are social and cultural processes that relate to our cultural identity. The way we see the world is part of our identity. Identity is the filter through which we present ourselves to the world. Literacy practices at home and at school link with students' evolving sense of themselves as cultural agents. How can teachers respond to this? When we teach language, there may be a clash between our students' identities and the curriculum we are required to teach. It is often in our identity that these differences emerge. When students interact with language, their identity infuses that language. When students grow up in homes and communities, they carry with them shared cultural spaces, the Church, the movies and the habits that their homes and communities engage with.

STUDIES OF IDENTITY AND LITERACY

Many studies have examined how identity informs literacy practices. Donna Alvermann explored how adolescents engaged in multiple, complex practices in order to explore identities (Alvermann, 2002). Moje, in her study, found that music and rap contributed to the literacy practices which young people could bring into classrooms (Moje et al., 2004). Luke and Carrington have looked at young children, and their 'glocalized' literacy practices, which need to be acknowledged in classroom settings (Luke and Carrington, 2002). Bartlett and Holland have looked at the space of literacy practices with regard to the stigma of illiteracy (Bartlett and Holland, 2002). Students have ideas and experiences that they bring with them from other places. These are inscribed into their literacy practices and travel with them.

In this chapter the following questions will be addressed:

1   Does a greater understanding of student identity inform literacy teaching?
2   How does our language use and language learning change when we move across sites?
3   Does our identity materialize in the multimodal texts we produce?
4   What is the relationship between identity and space?
5   What is the relationship between identity and artefacts?

ACTIVITY

Who are you?

Every year during the first week of school, Marianna Diiorio asks her year six students at an urban elementary school to complete a project called, Who are you? The assignment grows out of a concept presented in a set of readers and asks students to talk about what makes them unique. To begin with, they answer such questions as:

What is your background?
Do you have brothers or sisters?
What is your favourite sport?
What do you like to do in your spare time?
What makes you happy?

She then asks them to show what makes you **you** by filling a brown paper bag with articles that represent who they are. The bag includes 5–10 items. For example, Marianna is of Italian heritage, so she places a pasta-chain necklace in her brown bag. Students then present their items and how they make you **you** to the class.

IDENTITIES IN PRACTICE: WHAT CHILDREN BRING TO THEIR TEXTS

In Chapter 2 we discussed 'the interest of the sign-maker' and we return to this notion, but changing the vantage point of our analysis. We argued that texts carry the motivations of the producer (child, songwriter, publisher, poet, and so on), or as Kress expresses it, texts are motivated signs. Materials we choose to make a text of any kind bespeaks our identity. Kress speaks of 'best ways' of representing meanings. In some circumstances, meanings are best expressed through words and pictures, whereas in others, movement or three dimensions might be preferable. Children's artefacts carry with them the choices they made during the process – why they opted for red sweeps of colour with a bit of green vs purple sweeps of colour with a bit of green. This image can be now recognized as an artefact of identity.

Whereas in Chapter 2 we discussed what the producer brings to the texts, in this chapter we consider what the text brings to the producer. That is, how in our literacy teaching can we build our planning, texts and practices around the identities of students in our classrooms? In this chapter, practical ideas will be combined with theory to give some answers. The identities our students bring to texts will be explored and seen as diverse, and grounded in many different social practices.

Tactics for foregrounding identity

Here are some ideas to try out in your classroom:

Interview students about their home literacy practices.

Cover a range of genres of texts and discuss how these texts differ from one another.

Discuss students' written and visual work as traces of their identities and interests.

Keep anecdotal notes or observations on how students seem to be learning words or how their reading and writing is progressing.

In planning, think about how you actually use language in the classroom, and reflect this back to students as you teach.

Have students take on identities in stories or novels they are reading and compare them with their own reactions (and then have them take on very different types of characters).

When you consider identity in students' texts, it helps to remember that texts are traces of social practices (Rowsell, 2000). When texts are formed, they retain traces of the social practices of the text-maker. In this way, identities can be discerned within texts. Students' texts may be multimodal, that is, they may involve drawing, gesture and talk. These multimodal texts retain traces of multimodal practices within them. The experience of absorbing other texts will seep into the texts students create. These other texts, such as movies, stories and other cultural experiences, are ways in which students can express or play out identities. For example, a student may insert a Nike logo into a text, or draw a football flag of their favourite team to locate identities in texts. Students may customize their folders and describe their identities through symbols and stickers which they arrange as an artefact of their identity in a textual form.

A particularly strong way of looking at identity is to focus on children's engagement with popular culture. In this vignette, a reading recovery teacher drew on her student's knowledge of popular culture to support his reading and to give him some recognition for what his out-of-school practices were bringing to his reading in school:

Vignette: Texts to meet communicative practices

As a Reading Recovery teacher, Brenda Stein Dsaldov 'follows a specific protocol for each 30-minute lesson, which includes familiar text reading (1–3 texts), a running record, working with magnetic letters (letter or word work), a writing session, a book introduction to a new book and a first read-through of a new book'. Brenda shared a literacy event with us of a year one student who was having trouble learning to read and write. His literacy events at home comprised videogames and watching television (he did not get much exposure to print materials). Brenda decided 'to stay away from traditional, contrived language texts' and to build on the sorts of stories Michael enjoyed based on what he knew about language so far. As Brenda phrased it, 'Michael's engagement with television and videogames were shaping his ability to deal with text as a literacy form'.

Brenda saw it as her job to teach him more about written texts and how they functioned. Brenda appreciated how Michael's connection to popular culture and his knowledge of the visual mode of communication could have been a way to integrate written language into his literate identity. Michael had his own way of making meaning, but it was not yet related to the medium of lettered representation. Brenda felt it was critical for her to step back from the framework of Reading Recovery to observe Michael make meaning and how it could interact with a Reading Recovery model. By focusing on the modes of communication and types of texts a child uses, Brenda finds that she can tailor a structured model like Reading Recovery to student needs. To Brenda, the task of choosing appropriate texts is influenced by a consideration of how the child makes sense of the world around them through representations that they make. A text should represent some elements of the child's value system.

HOW CAN STUDENTS' IDENTITIES BE EXPLORED IN CLASSROOMS?

There are ways within the classroom to mediate identity with curriculum. There can be meeting spaces as done here where a student's own identity in practice can be opened up and explored. One way is to identify a student's language needs based on what they know and what they have experienced. If we work within Moje's *third space*, we focus on how identities are made within, through and against available representations (Moje et al., 2004). You can encourage students to keep a reading log; if they are young, parents could be involved in the activity that charts every literacy event – at home and at school – they embark on.

As literacy teachers, we have to remember that children are limited to public spaces that are constructed for them and, importantly, these spaces operate on the basis that children have something *to do* within them. There are not many opportunities within classroom spaces to manifest or to celebrate student identities. My-Linh celebrated student identities by putting up digital photographs. In Val's classroom, she provides physical space for identities by exhibiting a 'Young People Speak Out' board. This log could be transferred to the classroom walls and could become subject for discussion about literacy practices in everyday life. Students could take disposable cameras home to record the reading activity that goes on in the home – on a computer, or reading the television schedules or football results.

By acknowledging your students' literacy practices, you are acknowledging their identities. These identities will then become more visible in the classroom. The space of the classroom and the walls and the physical environment can support your students' identities in practice. They can be encouraged to bring in from outside the classroom the identity markers they feel close to. For example, in one family literacy class, a Turkish child drew flags of Turkey, as identity markers. A project on Paul Klée led to young children drawing the flats they lived in, in the style of Klée. A discussion ensued about the geographies of space in the city.

Part of this work recognizes that identities can be expressed in artefacts, which can then cross sites. In the case of Fatih's bird texts, these could be returned to in the home space, as meaningful objects, and part of his identity in practice. He played with his cut-out birds, his mother called him 'little bird' and the bird represented himself as artefact. Fatih included the bird in many of his drawings.

In school, Fatih also drew birds. His birds were both flying birds and non-flying birds. He drew them in response to the story the class was reading, *The Ugly Duckling*, but also, as his special needs helper observed, as artefacts of his identity. The bird was able to fly into the classroom (see Chapter 3 for the image of his bird). Many students in classrooms bring with them a plethora of digital identities such as console games, Internet experiences, text messaging and other digitized media.

Donna Alvermann: Adolescents and literacies in a digital world
■

Donna Alvermann explores the significance of young people's engagement with digital technologies by taking into account how adolescents use information and communication technologies to negotiate meaning within a broad array of globally defined and self-defined literacy practices. Alvermann takes a situated perspective to youth culture, arguing for exploring how people act at particular times within particular contexts using various discourses. Young people in her studies represent themselves in multiple modes with digital photographs, video clips and animations. In this way, they manifest their identities through multimodal communicational systems which guide their understanding of language (Alvermann, 2002).

The approach in this book argues that teachers' practices in classrooms are social practices. They are mediated by the identities of teacher and student. When social practice involves literacy, we have described them as literacy practices. What is curriculum when thought about with this view? Curriculum needs to be a space where multiple identities are present.

Elizabeth Moje: Third Space
■

Elizabeth Moje draws on the concept of *funds of knowledge*, from Moll et al. (1992), plus Gee's concept of Discourses, to examine the different home and community knowledge bases and Discourses students bring to bear on classroom texts. She and her colleagues look at third space theory to see where students' identities and practices are realized. In third spaces, identities are recognized and upheld in literacy practices. Students' **cultural resources** from peers, families and communities, including virtual communities such as the Internet, were found to be a powerful fund of

▶

knowledge for learning in classrooms. Popular music, movies, television and magazines were particularly powerful. She argued that the young people in her study were active creators of third space, of hybrid Discourses, in their everyday and school practices (Moje et al. 2004).

Creating a third space in your classroom

1   Use graphics to organize knowledge.

2   Try to begin lessons and units with student experiences.

3   Have students create artefacts as a culminating assessment task.

4   As much as possible, have a community tie within assignments.

5   Have students always reflect on their own experiences when completing an assignment.

6   Teachers do not always have the answers — give students agency in teaching.

IDENTITIES IN ARTEFACTS: WHAT CHILDREN BRING TO ARTEFACTS

Identity can also be found within artefacts. Edward, a 5-year-old child, loved trains. His mother, Mary, was originally born in India, and came to the UK when she was a teenager. Her grandfather had worked on the Indian railways. Displayed in the family's glass cabinet were two trains. One was built by Mary's grandfather as a reminder of his function in working on the Indian railways. Figure 5.1 shows the train made by the grandfather, in a photograph taken by Edward. Edward also collected models of trains. He also took a photograph of a Mallard train model, which was from Edward's own train collection. Both artefacts upheld the identities of the mother and the child. Edward's ruling passion was trains. As he explored his interest, family narratives lay behind his stories (Pahl, 2002).

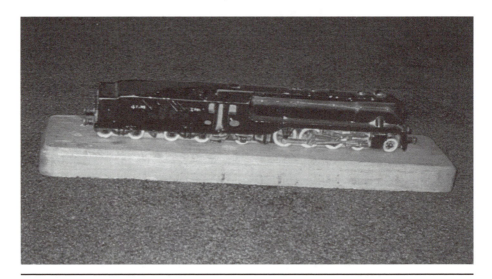

Figure 5.1 Indian train

Artefacts operate as powerful objects, which can become infused with identity. In homes these may be collectables, treasured objects, texts and pieces of the past, which accompany a family on its travels through time and space. Students who are victims of war, or come to a new country as refugees, are disconnected from the artefacts of their identity. By focusing on artefacts, powerful narratives of loss, displacement and migration can be uncovered.

Digitized artefacts, such as a console game, can also be infused with identity. Many games involve the construction of an *avatar*, an imaginary computer-generated icon which travels as the 'person' through the game. The player constructs an avatar in a game which then is used as an expression of identity. Children who play avatar-type games infuse their avatars with their own identity in practice (Pahl, 2005). Children could then slip in and out of these identities when playing games. For example, Sam, when playing a console game in his bedroom would announce, 'Whoops he got me' before slipping out of his 'role' as avatar to tell the researcher about his wobbly tooth:

> (*Sam was playing on his console game in his bedroom. I was watching him, and recording his comments as he played*).
>
> Sam: He's gotta get me one more time, or two more times
>   Oh man ate my supper!
>   Poha ... coming near me
>
> (*Sam's intonation totally changes from playground argot to 'mum' speak*)

Sam (to me):	Hey look
	Look
	I lost my teeth the other day
	I was worried that I swallowed it but/
Kate:	/What are you going to do with it?
Sam:	Put it under the pillow. (From Pahl, 2005)

This shift in identity, from tough 'fighting guy' to the child who had lost his tooth, is also a shift from being involved with the avatar Sam was playing with, to going into the 'real world' of his bedroom. The playing of videogames allows, as Gee commented, a 'projective identity' which children can use to become different identities and to move in and out of (Gee, 2003).

ACTIVITY

Artefacts tracing identity

Identify a way in which artefacts can be used by your students to talk about their identities. Clothing, for example, can be very powerful. Ask your class to talk about a favourite piece of clothing and use this to develop oral and then written narratives which can then be displayed on the walls alongside a photograph of the piece of clothing.

DISCURSIVE IDENTITY AND LITERACY: IDENTITY AND NARRATIVE

One way in which identity can be glimpsed is through stories. We tell stories about who we are and who we would like to be. Within narratives, identity can be glimpsed. Identities can be discursively upheld in stories. When people tell stories, their identities can be transformed or mediated, as they present to their audience a retold version of themselves. Stories can act as artefacts of identity, as a re-told story can be one in which a person 'finds themselves' and becomes transformed.

Dorothy Holland: Identities in Figured Worlds

Dorothy Holland argues that, 'People tell others who they are, but even more importantly, they tell themselves and then try to act as though they are who they say they are' (Holland et al., 2001: 3). Holland and colleagues argued that people *create* identities. They argue that identity is a concept

▶

> that works to connect the intimate or personal world with the wider world of social relations. Identities are located in 'figured worlds', which are spaces where social encounters are experienced and realized. They are collective 'as if' realms that can be experienced in narrative or through artefacts, which open up figured worlds. Holland's theory of identity rests on identities in practice being bound up with figured worlds. Identities are part of the accumulation of history, they are 'history in person'. (Holland et al., 2001; Lave and Holland, 2001)

When we consider our students, their experience is always represented in discourse. They have different identities for different communities they exist within. A child may speak a home language at home, and then English at school. These complex identities, which are connected to different sites, are part of who our students are. They may also encounter different 'figured worlds' through their out-of-school activities, including virtual worlds, play worlds, the worlds of popular culture and fantasy.

MULTIMODAL IDENTITY AND LITERACY

Much of the identity work our students do is enacted multimodally. It may be expressed through gesture, drawing, acting, 'performing' their identity in practice. This attention to multimodality opens up identity. Many students are constrained by a literacy curriculum that only allows writing.

In Elaine Millard's work on a **literacy of fusion**, students were encouraged to draw their 'Castle of Fear'. While some students drew *Harry Potter*-type objects in their castle, some drew objects from their own experience, such as a Hindi devil man or a lion (Millard, 2003). Multimodality can offer our students a way of negotiating and representing identities in the classroom.

Building multimodality into language planning and teaching

Questions to consider:

1   How do you define a multimodal text and how does it highlight different kinds of modes (that is, visual, gestural, audio, linguistic)?

2   How do pupils understand different modes within their tasks and which ones do they foreground?

3   How does identity play a role in multimodal choices within texts?

4   What is the best mode for a given assignment or subject area?

ACTIVITY

Thinking multimodally

Ask students to write about a particular website under multimodal headings. These would include the:

language,

sound,

visuals,

movement,

animation,

colour,

logos,

font

and any other interactive features. Then ask students to describe how they might design the website differently and why they foreground certain modes over others. As a critical framing and assessment activity, ask them to reflect on their choices and how it relates to their lived experience.

CONCLUSION

Finally, where can we locate teaching and learning within the new identities our students bring to our classrooms? Luke and Carrington argue that we need to fuse the local literacy practices our students engage with, with the global literacies they bring through the Internet, into a new 'glocalized' literacy, which can be used within curricula settings (Luke and Carrington, 2002). This form of literacy is the local infused with the global, and the global infused with the local. Each speaks to each other, and each has a relationship to each other.

Millard argues for a 'literacy of fusion' which combines multimodality with a focus on children's cultural resources and identities (Millard, 2003). This combines language and visual forms of representation. Moje argues for a 'third space' in which students' funds of knowledge are valued in hybrid spaces, and classroom knowledge is informed by home and community-based knowledge (Moje et al., 2004).

Schools can provide 'third spaces' which can enable students' identities to be recognized. This can bring in community interests, the ways in which the community works. Students' use of local community resources can be brought into the school. In the UK, extended or community schools acknowledge the diverse communities they serve (Nixon, Allan and Mannion, 2001). Family literacy classes can become spaces where families can bring cultural identities, family narratives and children's experience can be recognized and built upon in spaces which are neither classrooms or homes, but in-between spaces.

The role of creativity in literacy learning is hinged to identities and the way in which we learn is extended through creativity in learning. Students can be stretched in their learning as they use expressive language to write rap poems and learn to love language. In doing so, they use new vocabulary to develop new identities, as successful learners. Language becomes a tool for identity and for developing new identities.

Classrooms are spaces which can be infused with our students' identities. This is a challenge, to move the focus from the centre of the room to the circle around the room. Identities play a foundational role in our students' literacy development. When we speak, we enact our identity. As children come to write, the host of experiences they have had since birth are brought to bear on the writing processes. By recognizing and honouring that experience, we are bringing our students' identities into the classroom and, like Fatih's bird, letting them fly.

CHAPTER 6

Navigating New Literacies for New Times: Shaping Curriculum and Pedagogy

---

Vignette: Writing rap poetry in virtual worlds

Val Petersen's English class is aimed at students who were unable to pass their English examinations in secondary school. The course is delivered in a large college in a multi-ethnic city in the north of England. Students are taught their English course using an online platform, which delivers a series of units week by week, building up an understanding of English literature and language. The course is delivered online, together with face-to-face teaching. The course team decided to draw on the traditions of rap and hip-hop to deliver their course. In the course materials, rap music is used to understand concepts such as alliteration, assonance and metaphor. The students compare the work of rap artists with the work of William Blake.

The students meet weekly, in a real group. They are young people who have experienced school failure. Many are refugees from countries such as Somalia, and who have experienced a myriad of difficulties. Some are still living at home, others have left home, some live in foster homes. The course is called 'Young People Speak Out'.

The students are given a paper workbook to write in, plus have access to the course in an online form, in which they can put their answers up on the screen to particular questions. As the students learn and reflect on their materials, they text each other, exchange emails, discover other websites,

---

engage in instant-messaging systems, and play music on the CD-ROM. The websites they choose reflect their burgeoning cultural identities. A young Indian girl logs onto Asian Life and Bollywood Musicals. Students play music of their choice, R and B and rap.

When Val, the teacher, engages them in a discussion about identity and rap music, the students discuss with fervour and passion, and all work around one table. They converge, and then move back into their virtual online environments to write their own rap poetry. Val's teaching style invites students to reflect on the music they like, to disagree with one another, to work on English language and to be heard as equals within a classroom setting.

KEY THEMES IN THE CHAPTER

- *Curriculum, that is, what is taught, often inscribed in documents and disseminated and formed at national level*
- *Pedagogy, that is, the way in which the curriculum is interpreted and taught and the assumptions behind that teaching that guide and shape teachers' practices*

INTRODUCTION

Imagine a classroom that speaks to the needs and interests of *all* students in your classroom. A classroom that can work interchangeably in two and three dimensions (in print and in virtual worlds). A classroom that builds on home practices to inform school practices. A classroom that engages meaning-makers. It is a classroom at the interface of teacher identity and student identity *and* at practice/pedagogy and curriculum. It is the kind of classroom we want to create for our students.

This chapter takes a look at some of the most exciting and innovative curricula work around the world in literacy. It asks, what would the classroom of tomorrow look like?

- In the classroom of tomorrow, tasks that involve *problem-solving*, analysis and practices using print and visual, electronic, face-to-face media in combinations that are occurring in new, civic, media and workplace contexts are presented to students.

- They are given the opportunity to develop *critical literacies* skills, involving second-guessing, criticizing and arguing with a range of texts, and understanding their sources, production and power relations.

- Students engage in *collaborative work*, that involves collaborative reading, writing and decision-making in literacy events within and across learning communities.

- They engage in **intercultural communication** that involve negotiating and solving problems across cultures and languages, and understanding the residual and emergent traditions within one's own cultures.

- As language teachers, you will be situating your practice to suit contemporary needs; you will teach language overtly and encourage an understanding of embodied meanings. You will critically frame texts and their attendant practices; and, finally, you will exhibit transformed practice where students are engaged, interested and on task. Future classrooms involve both *global and local* analyses: that involve understanding the diversity and sundry funds of knowledge our students bring to the classroom (Luke, 2002).

In this chapter, we consider what the classroom of tomorrow could look like, but in doing so we draw on the teaching practices of today, using examples from teaching situations in different contexts. We return to many of the themes in previous chapters: communities of learners/communities of practice; identities/positioning; and the role of power/status in literacy teaching. We want to argue for a critical literacy that envisions literacy as a tool for re-mediating one's relation to the global flows of capital and information. We ask these questions:

- What can the ideas of the New Literacy Studies give teachers?

- How can they actively make sense of them in their own settings?

The approach in this book tells us that teachers' practices in classrooms are social practices. When they involve literacy, they can be described as literacy practices. The literacy curriculum you teach is constructed in relation to social practice and assumptions about literacy.

Curricula are shaped by theories of how literacy is taught. Often, they are shaped by what kind of literacy is thought to be important. In many countries, literacy is seen as a set of transferable skills, to be transferred and disseminated. Curricula are shaped by power. What is taught, and how it is taught is often determined by people in governments who would like to see students learn a particular form of literacy.

Think about how this applies in your case.

Questions to critically frame practice:

What is taught (that is, the contents of the syllabus you deliver to your students)?

What teaching methods do you use?

Whom do you teach and where are the classes located?

What aspects of the curriculum are assessed?

Who are the assessors?

How do they assess?

ACTIVITY

Questions to consider

Why is the curriculum constructed in the way it is?

Who constructs and/or has influence on your curriculum?

Who benefits from the curriculum?

WHAT IS COVERED IN THIS CHAPTER

In this chapter examples of innovative curricula and pedagogy will be discussed from a range of settings. These include:

- family literacy programmes (classes where parents and children learn together, often held in school settings);

- schools (nursery, infant, junior and secondary schools);

- post-16 provision for young people and adults.

In addition, there will be examples of places where the curriculum has been changed, both at government level and within particular settings, schools or classrooms. These include examples from:

- Australia;

- South Africa;

- the USA;

- Canada;

- the UK.

Different levels of curricula innovation will be discussed. These include:

■ *macro-level* curricula change – this includes change at government level;

■ *meso-level* curricula change – this includes change at school administration level;

■ *micro-level* curricula change – this includes change at teacher and classroom level.

In this chapter, we focus on the micro. We consider how you, as a teacher within the classroom, can mediate your curriculum so that the literacy practices of your students can become incorporated into your teaching. Specific examples will be given to aid you in that process. *Your voice, as teacher, is the voice we listen to in this chapter.*

THEORIES OF NEW CURRICULUM IN NEW TIMES

In the vignette that begins the chapter, students are navigating new pathways across a number of different literacies. In some cases, they engage in traditional, writing-based activities, such as when they fill in worksheets on different sounds used in a rap song, to demonstrate an understanding of assonance. In other cases, they are working using a keyboard. However, they also listen to music, or send text messages. They access websites and develop ways of moving in and out of different virtual spaces. Sometimes they move from listening to a CD, to reading the words on the paper, and then writing their own words after discussion. In some cases, they are engaged in virtual chat, while working on their task online, while text messaging. They are working in a multimodal environment. These sorts of practices have been described by Colin Lankshear and Michele Knobel in their book, *New Literacies*.

Lankshear and Knobel: New literacies

Lankshear and Knobel use a number of different examples to describe how the nature of literacy is changing with digitization. They describe how teenagers create personal web diaries, called *weblogs* to chart ideas and develop personal identities. They describe how the trading environment of eBay changed literacy practices and how identities online were affected by the eBay ratings system. They argue that attention is a feature of the new digital literacies: they involve a change in the economies of attention, as much digitized media requires different kinds of attention, on a different

---

▶

scale. Equally, ways of knowing in relation to the new literacies, and the digitized environment, are different. Sometimes, the children we teach know more than us, and have different ways of knowing. These ways of knowing need to be recognized in the classrooms of tomorrow (Lankshear and Knobel, 2003).

Vignette: Learning journals

Anjana is a student on an ICT-based Family Learning program called 'Keeping up with the Children'. This is based in the nursery her son attends in an outer suburb of London. She has a young child, and wants to know how she can support him at nursery. The course introduces parents to how their children learn, and encourages parents to observe their own children and, using digital cameras, record their learning journeys. These are particular learning experiences that can be documented. Staff use this framework as a form of assessment, gradually building up a picture of what each child can achieve within the nursery setting. The Family Learning class is double-staffed, with a teacher from the nursery and a tutor who focuses on the adults' literacy skills.

Using the concept of the 'learning journey', the tutor develops an activity by which Anjana can write PowerPoint slides, with images from a digital camera, detailing her son's learning journeys in the nursery. The slides show her son playing in the sandpit and enjoying water play as part of his curricula activities. Anjana takes the CD-ROM home, where she works on them on her home computer.

Anjana progressed onto a further course to support her literacy. As part of the nursery curriculum, the children were learning about cultural and religious festivals. At New Year, the children investigated festivals around the world. One part of the course was looking at the Chinese New Year. Anjana returned with information on her PowerPoint about her own New Year celebrations, from India, her country of origin. As a result, through the CD-ROM and with support from the family literacy tutor and the nursery staff, Anjana used PowerPoint to write about her own cultural experience.

This example blends the use of new technologies, which then enable a home–school continuum. She is taking her experience from home to school, inscribed in the PowerPoint presentation. The technology supports the sharing of experience, in this case, the festivals from China and India around the New Year. The student also follows her son's learning journeys and records them in her PowerPoint presentation. Anjana has designed a learning experience for herself, independently, at home and then developed her work with the support of her tutor and the nursery workers. She has also contributed to her son's assessment framework, using new technologies and information from home.

How can Anjana's learning be inscribed in a curriculum of the future? She has designed her own multimodal document, on screen, using images from a digital camera. These images are used for a PowerPoint presentation, which is then printed out and used as a display in the nursery and at conferences. She has brought her own cultural experience to this activity, and also contributed to an assessment framework for her son. This is an example of micro curricula innovation, but supported by the nursery and the Family Learning team at a meso level, that is school level. The project was documented at a macro level, as the project attracted funding from a National Agency in the UK, the Basic Skills Agency, which was then evaluated in a report (Pahl, 2004b).

Cope and Kalantzis: Multiliteracies revisited
■

Here, we remind you that as described in Chapter 4, the **multiliteracies** curriculum starts from the insight that learning is multimodal. It envisages pedagogy as a complex integration of four factors:

- *situated practice* which involves students drawing on the world of learners' experiences of design and designing;
- *overt instruction* which involves learners shaping a language of design;
- *critical framing*, which relates meanings to their social contexts and purposes;
- *transformed practice* in which students transfer their designs of meaning from one context to another (Cope and Kalantzis, 2000).

If we describe Anjana's activity using the concepts from Multiliteracies, it is possible to understand the process. She draws on her *situated practice* of using PowerPoint and learning from her son and the nursery he attends to shape a new text: her son's learning journal presentation. She is then informed by *overt instruction* from the teacher which enables her to shape her presentation. Her work is subsequently informed by a *critical framing*, when she looks at what she knows in connection with the curricula in the nursery. This leads to *transformed practice*. This is the new text she has created with the help of her teachers and the technology. She then draws on her own cultural experience to add to her presentation with an account of the Indian New Year along with her son's experience of the nursery's discussion of the Chinese New Year. This is transformed through her work on the CD-ROM and represented in the nursery context.

In the above vignette, Anjana has drawn on her own experience, her fund of knowledge from home. In many examples in this book, experiences from home have been used to further students' literacy in school settings. In the example at the start of the chapter, students brought their prior cultural experience of rap music with them into the classroom. This was used to develop their literacy skills, and was drawn on when composing and writing. This idea of drawing on what children bring to writing has been developed in a number of areas.

- In Graham's *writing journals*, students drew on experiences of playing console games to compose multi-layered texts, which drew on the structure of the game to represent the console game, in this case Spiderman, in a series of drawings. This was part of a writing project which supported children to compose, using drawing or writing, texts of their choice in the classroom (Graham, 2004).

- In the *Shoebox project*, described at the start of Chapter 3, children filled a shoebox with artefacts from home. These artefacts were used to support children in composing and in delivering oral narratives in classroom settings (Feiler et al., in press).

- A *bilingual course for parents*, described in Chapter 3, involved parents telling their children stories from their own cultures, and then making a video with them for their children to listen to and use to develop their language and literacy skills (Pahl, 2004b).

ANOTHER LOOK AT FUNDS OF KNOWLEDGE AND THIRD SPACE

How can these different examples of practice be linked to theory? Once again, these examples can be linked to Moll's concept of *funds of knowledge*. This research emphasizes the importance of what students and communities bring to schools in terms of literacy practices (Moll et al., 1992). These models see out-of-school literacy practices as flowing into school and developing within classrooms.

These everyday understandings can be channelled into different forms of knowledge. Moll and then Gutiérrez and others have suggested that students' cultural resources can be viewed as resources for helping students develop stronger understandings of the natural world, both in classrooms and everyday lives (Gutiérrez et al., 1999). As seen in Chapter 5, the term *third space* can be used to describe a bridge between community/home ways of speaking and reading and writing, and school-based literacy practices. This third space is a space where students can be supported to move their literacy practices into a schooled domain of knowledge. From this theory, many researchers have thought about what could be used from everyday literacy practices to support school knowledge. To return to the rap vignette at the beginning of this chapter, the knowledge of rap music students brought to the classroom was then transformed and applied to examine the poetry of William Blake.

How do we transform our students' funds of knowledge in classroom settings? Teachers can mediate classroom experiences for their students, bringing in a host of cultural experience from their students' funds of knowledge, and they can meet their students halfway with a shared space in which both can participate.

Bringing students' life experiences into the classroom

How can students' life experiences be brought into the classroom? It is possible to do this in relation to students:

- as writers;
- as readers.

This example looks at how students bring their life experiences into the classroom as **readers**. One idea of how to bring in students' life experience would be for the teacher and students to bring their funds of knowledge to bear upon a specific text. This has been called a **reader response** view of reading stories. Reader response theories recognize that readers use their life experience, and their cultural identities to make meaning from texts. In the reader response classroom, students are active participants in constructing meaning from texts. This means that students' interpretations of stories are recognized as valid.

In one study, teachers decided that this concept did not go far enough in exploring how the reader's identity is positioned with regard to the text. For example, a girl reading a text about a macho gang culture will read it differently from a boy. A critical reading project would allow for these complexities (McDonald, 2004). In an

▶

Australian critical reading project, children were encouraged to become critical readers, who could identify texts as crafted objects, and who were alert to the values and interests which texts carry within them and how some invite readers in and others are more difficult (McDonald, 2004).

In order to look at texts, a critical literacy lens is useful. This lens might think about ways in which texts create assumptions and develop ideologies.

Applying a critical literacy lens

Look for deeper understanding in texts (How do I crack this code?).

Examine the purpose of a text (What does this mean?).

Suggest — with texts of all kinds — that texts are not neutral (Who wrote this text?).

Analyse power in texts (for example, the difference between a student website and Microsoft Word's website) (Whose authority lies beneath this text?).

Emphasize multiple perspectives on the same issue (If this were written by someone else, how would it be different?).

Provide students with opportunities to examine different genres of texts (If this were in a different genre, what would it be like?).

Provide students with opportunities for social action (How does this relate to me?).

As readers and writers we engage with texts in a fashion which is personal and ideological. We are not value-free. By looking at what lies beneath texts, we acknowledge the way in which these texts are traces of social practice. The texts are constructed by agencies and people, and developed over a time frame. Sometimes texts can be identified with particular, more settled forms, which we recognize in everyday life; for example, formal letters or newspaper articles. At other times, texts are unstable and can move rapidly in and out of speech like forms of text and more written forms of text. Weblogs, for example, move between informal discourse and more formal written forms.

ACTIVITY

Keeping a log

Make a log of your reading for one day. Include books, bus timetables and any trivia you encounter. Notice how you **feel** about each bit of reading you do. At the end of the day, reflect on which reading materials you enjoyed, which you disliked. Write the title, 'My secret life of reading' on a piece of paper.

What did that activity tell you about your reading? Has it given you a sense of what the meaning of the text has told you? How do some texts grab your attention and not others? Consider whether, if a text has visuals such as a magazine, or a particular perspective which you may agree with, this helps you enjoy a text more.

REFLECTION

Now consider how you could use this activity in the classroom. How could you devise a questionnaire which could find out about your students' reading habits? Would it help to use cameras for them to record their home reading habits? Could you ask for your students to use their mobile phones to text their responses back to you – possible with teenagers. In asking your students to record their out-of-school reading habits, you can then invite them to display and articulate these in the classroom. How would this activity support your students' reading within the classroom?

CURRICULUM, TEXTS AND LITERACY PRACTICES

The shaping of the new curriculum needs to respond to the new pathways our students take through, 'globalised and local, virtual and material social fields' (Luke and Carrington, 2002: 233). In the new modern world of clicking, societies connect virtually, and there is increased speed of economic movement across the globe. The way information is presented is changing and moving, as states' boundaries blur. Increased inequalities in urban spaces make it more urgent to harness the skills of young people to education and to foster their literacy development. Out-of-school literacies that researchers have documented include:

- weblogs;

- console-games playing;

- looking up 'cheats ' on the Internet for games playing;

- playing online games;

- communicating with others in online chatrooms;

- text messaging;

- bidding on eBay;

- surfing the Web;

- constructing online identities and relating to different people online.

How can the curriculum respond to these changing times and changing textual practices?

In this section, some examples of how teachers have mediated the curriculum are given. In particular, we focus on the following examples drawing on students':

- home literacy practices;

- multimodal practices;

- new literacies, especially digitized literacies;

- critical literacies.

DRAWING ON STUDENTS' HOME LITERACY PRACTICES

Researching your students brings in information about their literacy practices. This then can be used to construct the curriculum. Here are some ideas:

- *Using maps to locate students' home spaces*: information about students' geographies can be used to map their worlds. Children can draw maps of their home environments. They can then describe in words what different spaces meant to them and where they play.

- *Using a multimodal approach to research*: a multimodal approach lets in more meanings. Children can describe their games playing and television-watching through drawings and modelling.

- *Using the alphabet to trigger home meanings*: you can use the alphabet with young children to prompt words which mean something to them. These can be made into books to support early reading.

- *Bring in artefacts to trigger memories and stories*: drawings and artefacts can be brought in from home to support writing. Children's home narratives can be structured around artefacts. These can act as a way of signalling identities and memories.

- *Use disposable cameras to record home practices*: photographing home literacy practices can be used as a prompt to literacy in the classroom. A display can be made of what children recorded with their cameras.

- *Draw on children's popular culture*: Drawing on popular culture in the classroom can bring in fresh ideas and can motivate and inspire children. For example, students can record themselves singing their favourite pop songs, describe the playing of a console game in drawing and writing, or tell stories, or create drama drawing on favourite television programmes.

- *Students as researchers*: your students can also carry out the research themselves. As researchers, they become involved in recording and noticing their literacy practices.

In the following example, teachers used visual research methods to find out what literacy practices children engaged with.

Vignette: Investigating home literacy practices

In a small-scale research project, two groups of primary school children were involved in investigating the use of literacy in their lives, using disposable cameras to record literacy events and texts. These photographs generated discussion and reflection on what the children found. The researchers found that the children used literacy:

- *as a way of maintaining and reinforcing relationships;*
- *as a means of organizing life;*
- *as a vehicle for learning;*
- *as reflection of identity;*
- *for private pleasure (Burnett and Myers, 2002: 57).*

These understandings were then used to enrich teachers' understandings of the children's literacy practices, and were used in classroom activities.

The use of research as a tool for enriching classrooms has been used in many settings. One very simple way to find out about your students' home literacy practices is to observe them as they work and talk. Studies have recorded students' talk outside the classroom and in the classroom collected children's texts both in and out of the classroom and followed children from home and school and back again. These studies have enriched classroom practice.

REFLECTION

The efficacy of observation

Observation as a tool is rich in possibilities. While we cannot probe the psyche, we can use techniques such as observation and analysis of the things children make to give us insights about how thought is structured, as well as how the social organization of the world appears to the child (Pahl, 1999).

Finding out about your students' home literacy practices allows an understanding of the changing nature of literacy. If your students use text messaging, play on games consoles, engage in instant messaging, email or weblogs, these are all new literacy practices which can be drawn upon in classroom practice.

ASSESSING NEW LITERACY STUDIES THROUGH PORTFOLIOS

To assess your students' literacy development when working within a New Literacy Studies or multiliteracies framework, students can be encouraged to create a portfolio as an effective way of encouraging them to invest in the literacy process. At the beginning of the year, each student receives a portfolio that they can decorate however they like. As a culminating assessment task, ask students to divide their portfolio into sections as a collection of assignments. For example, students can provide an assignment or artefact that exhibits proficiency in speaking, listening, writing, reading and **visual communication**. Structuring portfolios in relation to the themes drawing on theory from multiliteracies, such as 'best design' or 'best piece of writing within a genre', helps students develop a greater understanding of the ways of understanding the possibilities and constraints of contemporary curricula and activities that can grow out of the New Literacy Studies. For example, students can present artefacts that illustrate home–school literacy practices, multimodal literacies, multiliteracies or artefacts of their identity.

Another way of structuring the portfolio process might be based on text genres: fiction, poetry, websites, non-fiction, videogames or game cards, and so on. Portfolio note headings can reflect the learning process by looking at:

- What I knew;

- What I wanted to find out;

- What I found out.

Students reflect on the process of creating artefacts to consolidate their learning. These reflections appear in each portfolio section. Portfolios represent informal forms of assessment that allow students to take ownership of their literacy development while at the same time drawing on ideas from the New Literacy Studies, such as the idea of literacy as a social practice.

DRAWING ON STUDENTS' MULTIMODAL PRACTICES

Eve Bearne (2003) argued that it is possible to recognize how children draw on different *affordances* in relation to their texts. Affordances are the possibilities within texts to create meaning. Some affordances may be located in language and literacy, that is, they may be found in written texts. Some may, however, be drawn, but spatially organized to add to the writing. Bearne argued that we need to credit these spatial assemblages of thought, to create, in Elaine Millard's words, 'a literacy of fusion' – one that combines an understanding of literacy in relation to reading and writing with an understanding of literacy in relation to images (Millard, 2003). Multimodality can be used within the classroom in a variety of ways to support students' learning. Returning to the multiliteracies project, Cope and Kalantzis describe the following classroom vignette:

> *Back to Australia again, and this time to William Ross High School in Townsville, North Queensland. This is another of the schools with which we were working in our Language Australia/ARC project. Here Fran Hodges is working with her Year 9 English class on video clips. She starts by presenting the students with the lyrics of a Toni Childs' song. All the devices and conventions of poetry are to be found, as well as the specific conventions of song lyrics, such as a repeated chorus. Then she plays the CD. She asks what the music adds to the lyrics and how it does it. Then she plays the video clip. She*

asks how the imagery of the clip and gestures of the singer add to the meaning of the song. The students have now completed an analysis of the multimodal grammar of the song. Next, the students bring in their favourite songs. Situated practice: *students bring music they relate to in their own life experience and immerse themselves in the music of their friends.* Overt instruction: *Fran works with the students as they develop a grammar which analyses the linguistic, audio and visual design of the songs and their video clips.* Critical framing: *students compare the meanings and the cultures they represent – the song of the white woman (Toni Childs) rap, techno, house, reggae, heavy metal or whatever.* Transformed practice: *the students write, perform and make a video clip for a song they have written themselves.* (Cope and Kalantzis, Putting Multiliteracies to the Test)

Vignette: Filming narratives

In Sandra Cheng's year 2 class in an inner city primary school, she has found a way of assessing children's oral language by recording her students' narratives. At different points in the year, Sandra videotapes students as they retell a story they have read. She then downloads it through I-movie and sits through a screen-by-screen play with colleagues to analyse the retelling abilities of students. She stores the videos on her computer and revisits them as the year progresses.

In these examples, new technology opens up a different space for students to explore different identities in practice and to become experts within a New Literacies framework. Low-achieving students can then adopt different identities within the classroom.

Vignette: Using PowerPoint to present a slide show about the English department

In a classroom in Bristol, UK, a group of teachers worked with 15–16-year-old students with low to high literacy skills to produce PowerPoint slides for a parents' evening. The presentation would promote the work of the English department. The pupils designed the presentation drawing on colour and font, and organizing the layout of the slides in order to present information. The pupils downloaded and selected effective images from the Web, animated the presentation, drew on digital pictures and used informal and dramatic commands to inject humour into their presentation. In doing so, they showed an understanding of audience and impact. By show-

▶

> *ing awareness of a multimodal design element to the work, the pupils were given credit for the complexity they showed in putting the presentation together. Students with low literacy skills, nonetheless, demonstrated a keen awareness of design, audience and presentation in the PowerPoint slide project* (Mathewman, 2004).

DRAWING ON STUDENTS' NEW LITERACIES

In some places, the curriculum has been reshaped to support new literacies. For example, a group of researchers worked with a school in Australia to assist with the under-achievement of certain groups in the school. A core of 25 per cent of the children in the school struggled with literacy difficulties. The researchers did an audit of the skills these students already had, and discovered they had strong social networks within the community, in-depth local knowledge about the demography and culture of their own community, interest in money and sports, and how to deal with difficult economic circumstances (Luke and Carrington, 2002). They also had extensive knowledge of popular culture, music, fashion and youth culture, computer and video games, Internet surfing and the new technologies. The researchers worked with the teachers to audit and develop classroom strategies which built on these strengths. The researchers worked to bring together, 'a richer, more intellectually demanding and "contemporary" analysis of these kids' identities and competencies, a more cogent understanding of the overlapping and multiple communities that these children inhabit with a balanced focus on code breaking, meaning making, using texts in everyday life and critical literacy' (Luke and Carrington, 2002: 243).

The new curriculum could take a number of shapes including:

- using the Internet to audit and to analyse global flows of work;

- using writing and online communication to participate with virtual communities linked to current interests;

- reading multiple literary texts that generate or engage intercultural and contrastive historical perspectives (Luke and Carrington, 2002: 247).

Curricula change could focus on both the local and the global, drawing on children's identities and interests, and allowing a space for them to grow and develop that is at once, embedded and inclusive.

> ### Vignette: Documenting multiliteracies
>
> In Toronto and Vancouver, Canada, a group of researchers are document-
> ing initiatives in the Toronto and Vancouver school systems that focus on
> multiliteracies. Through case studies, the study will identify characteristics
> and practical conditions that need to be in place to create a multiliteracies
> classroom. The study will tie their work on designing classrooms and plan-
> ning and implementing multiliteracies programmes with assessment
> policies, including large-scale standardized tests, that are in use in both
> provinces. As well, the team of researchers hope to analyse how school
> leadership, community and university partnerships, and teacher education
> can work together to implement a multiliteracies approach to the teaching
> of literacy. The project therefore covers the three main domains of school:
>
> ■ **macro** (how governments can embed multiliteracies in their curricula);
>
> ■ **meso** (how school leaders can build their literacy initiatives around a
>   multiliteracies framework);
>
> ■ **micro** (how teachers can apply multiliteracies in their classroom – and
>   the resources they will need to do so).
>
> The study proposes to articulate the choices that school systems face with
> respect to what forms of literacy to teach and what pedagogical options
> are most appropriate for teaching different forms of literacy (Cummins et
> al., 2002).

DRAWING ON STUDENTS' CRITICAL LITERACIES

In South Africa, the Multiliteracies Project was implemented both as a ped-
agogic practice and as a curriculum document. What this meant in practice
is that teachers were encouraged in their training to draw on the diverse
representational resources of their students. The following examples were
given: 'One student began work on a multi-media CD Rom aimed at developing children's environmental awareness in under-resourced local
communities. Another student devised a workbook on oral storytelling
practices for Tsonga-speaking children, where students had to compare and
contrast different English translations of a well-known Tsonga oral narrative' (Newfield and Stein, 2000: 295).

Part of the teachers' work in developing a critical framing for their students
was a pedagogy which invited students in as 'experts' and allowed them
space within the pedagogical setting they were in. The combining with critical literacies with multimodality meant that students who were experts in
oral and visual modes could apply this knowledge in a curricula context.

Assessing critical literacy development

To assess students' critical literacy development, you can apply the following criteria:

1 Meaning-making is use of all resources possible in their production of texts (that is, enabling/affording vs constraining meaning based on the genre). Do they know the practices required to build and construct cultural meanings in texts?

2 The text participant is making meaning from texts. Students then ask, what does this mean?

3 The text user is cracking the 'code' of the text, and accessing the embodied meanings in a text. How can we look at what lies beneath the text?

4 A text analyst has proficiency in the practices required to analyse, critique, and second-guess texts. How can we empower students to apply critical literacies skills to texts?

PEDAGOGY AND THE NEW LITERACY STUDIES

Finally, this chapter looks at pedagogy. How can a pedagogy invite students' home experiences, and their expertise in digital literacies and multimodality, into the classroom? It is important to recognize the schooled literacy pedagogy is in itself a literacy practice. We need to invite our students to ask the questions:

- Why is the type of literacy associated with schooling come to be so powerful?

- Can we consider other forms of literacy in curricula documents?

- What forms would they take?

We have made strides in applying New Literacies in our thinking, policy and practice, but we need to change our mindset to affect pedagogy.

Joanne Larson and Lyn Gatto proposed a pedagogy of **tactics**. From de Certeau, they draw on the concept of strategies and tactics.

De Certeau on shaping space and practice

Strategies are institutional, spatial and ideological practices used by producers and consumers in the course of everyday life.

Strategies are the way the powerful shape space and practices through bureaucratic measures such as standardized assessments and mandated curricula.

> *Tactics* are the ways the people who live within institutionalized spaces use, manipulate and divert the space to which they are assigned (De Certeau, 1984: 18; Larson and Gatto, 2004: 14).

Larson described how in Gatto's classroom, she adopted strategies to develop a curriculum based on a shared knowledge and Discourse with her students (Larson and Gatto, 2004: 19). At the same time, Gatto's students drew on tactics to negotiate and renegotiate classroom structures (Larson and Gatto, 2004: 19). Gatto allowed students into the knowledge spaces of the classroom and arranged the space so that her desk was a child-size desk that sits amongst the children. Gatto's students designed the environment and Gatto supported a team concept which radically shifted power relations in her classroom (Larson and Gatto, 2004: 23). The students perceived this vibrant learning community as fun. Larson and Gatto write that,

> *The children are given opportunities to negotiate rules, discipline procedures, and instructional routines. Simply offering children choice is not necessarily sufficient to transform power relations. We argue that by shifting responsibility for learning to the team, Gatto does more than 'give' choice; she asks students to take responsibility for co-constructing their own learning.* (Larson and Gatto, 2004: 23)

Gatto used video, filming children for them to watch and reflect on, as a resource for children to understand how their actions affect people in the community, and students are encouraged to participate in new experiences outside their neighbourhood communities. Children are asked to question everything, and to actively engage in problem-solving.

Vignette: Making family books

Sally Kelly's family learning class for CETS in Croydon was set in a primary school in a multilingual suburban community with a long history of parental involvement and a family learning room. The course involved 13 bilingual parents who worked together to develop family books for their children. The headteacher saw the course as building community links, and thought it was a wonderful dimension to her school. The tutor found that students who attended the class built friendship bonds, enriched their social lives, and felt more confident with the school. The course focused on visits to museums and art and craft. Parents as well as children worked on the production of family books which each child and parent worked on together. These books contained stories from the families, their family tree and where they were from and using dual language, in the student's home languages, to tell stories.

Sally's approach to the students was to value them. She encouraged them to name the months of the year in their own languages and translate other information in the books made together with their children. Students came from a number of different linguistic backgrounds, including Urdu, Punjabi, Bengali, Albanian, Hindi, Marathi, Tamil, Kurdish and Gujurati speakers. The students drew on their own linguistic resources, including their older children, some of whom were learning Urdu at school, to name particular months and seasons.

Sally also incorporated a design element into her curriculum. She drew on the art skills of the children and the parents, who decorated the family books they made and encouraged parents to work in clay and to experiment with different materials, which were then displayed. By focusing on design, she supported the parents in a diversity of skills. The children were assessed and improved in language and fine motor skills after the course. Fozia was very proud of her family book (Figure 6.1).

Fig 6.1 Fozia's family book

PEDAGOGY AS MEDIATING PRACTICE ACROSS MICRO, MESO AND MACRO LEVELS

This example combines a number of pedagogical factors to support students' home literacy practices. Sally focused on friendship amongst the students as one of her learning goals. She encouraged students to write in dual languages when labelling particular images. She developed her students' language skills alongside the visual and design elements, and valued both equally. Supported at meso level by the school administration, who provided a family learning room for the class, and a well-staffed crèche for younger children, the course had wide learning outcomes. For example, the classroom teacher who worked with the children recognized that the children's drawing skills had improved as a result of the course. Equally, language skills had improved. At macro level, Sally's course was enshrined in an accreditation system, written by Sally herself, but nationally recognized across boundaries. The mediating of the pedagogy, Sally's valuing of her students, ensured the motivation and success of the course. Part of the success lay in the recognition of her students' identities

Likewise, in the vignette at the head of this chapter, Val used a particular pedagogical style to invite her students to reflect on language. She did not shut out her students' experiences of surfing the Net, and listening to music, but allowed them within the classroom. Her classroom became an equitable space, where young people's voices were heard. She mediated pedagogy in micro ways, through asking students for their advice when composing text on an interactive whiteboard. She was supported at meso level through the English online team's development of the online course. Finally, at macro level, the course became part of a research project, and was externally funded for evaluation.

CONCLUSION

In this chapter, ideas for a new curriculum and pedagogy have been put forward. Starting from the idea of students' changing literacy practices, the chapter argues for an investigation into students' out-of-school literacies as the starting point for a new curriculum. Changing literacy practices require changing instructional modes. The mutliliteracies pedagogy suggests a shift to the idea of design and to the assessment of design as a way of moving beyond a linguistically based curriculum. By focusing on critical literacies, the literacy practices of different cultures can be considered in relation to issues of power and control. Finally, mediation through a pedagogy, which recognizes that students use tactics and teachers use strategies to implement curricula, can alert us to where there is room for change. By looking at pedagogy through the lens of micro, meso and macro, there can be opportunities to link the micro to the macro and see where new pedagogical structures can be supported by the meso, or school administration level.

At the heart of this chapter is hope. Hope that the children of tomorrow will be given space to learn in a pedagogical setting which respects their literacy practices, and affords them instruction which draws on those practices. This requires the development of an equitable classroom. Hope also that teachers are given the support to give their students this space, and are themselves given space as the mediators of the curriculum of tomorrow. This requires a flexible and adaptable curriculum. This chapter also hopes that the micro practices we have observed in classrooms in London, Sheffield, Croydon, Derbyshire, Toronto and Newfoundland may be enshrined in the macro curricula documents of the twenty-first century.

Conclusion: Literacy Today ... and Tomorrow

We are educating our students in a time when local literacies are at odds with government perspectives on literacy education. As we plan, teach, and assess our students' literacy development, we are mediating macro, meso and micro systems. That is, we are mediating the government (macro), the school administration (meso) and classroom curricula (micro). Teachers engage with all three levels in their work.

We are teaching at a time of change, of movement and of migration, and of tremendous shifts in our communicative practices. Our students learn how to read and write in this diversified space, facing the incongruities of home practices like weblogging and schooling practices like taking a role in a literature circle. It is hardly surprising that we face policy initiatives and district-wide interventions to contend with falling literacy rates and school closures.

In the past, although there were shifts in pedagogy and accepted practice, literacy education was fairly predictable in that the medium (printed texts) remained the same and ways or styles of using them shifted, but they were manageable and ameliorated current practice. For example, **genre theory** moved us forward in understanding, on ideological and practical levels, the importance of the form and function of texts in developing a knowledge and proficiency with language. In the present and future, however, stabilizing factors like the reading scheme have been usurped by a plethora of print and digital texts.

Changes in our **communicational landscape** were anticipated by such theorists as Marshall McLuhan and Raymond Williams whose prescient writings on the revolutionary nature of television, film and technology have been realized today (McLuhan, 1964; Williams, 2001). As Williams observed in *The Long Revolution*:

> We 'see' in certain ways – that is, we interpret sensory information according to certain rules – as a way of living. But these ways – these rules and interpretations – are, as a whole, neither fixed not constant. We can learn new rules and new interpretations, as a result of which we shall literally see in new ways. (Williams, 2001: 34)

Williams argued that each generation comes anew to communication and to culture, and new generations, 'never talk quite "the same language" as the one before' (Williams, 2001: 64). Above all, Williams argued that, 'the new generation will have its own structure of feeling' (Williams, 2001: 65). It is this change we must recognize in our students.

To cope with the reality of not only technology but also immigration and new linguistic systems in our local worlds, we have to merge and mediate models that are both familiar and foreign, or viewed another way, comfortable and intimidating.

Vignette: Molly and the home–school divide

Molly is 6 years old. She has difficulty with her reading and writing and shows little interest in print texts like Three Little Pigs *which are sent home on a weekly basis in her book bag. For homework, she is asked to study high frequency words and work on her spelling. In sharp contrast, at home, Molly likes to draw or paint with her family, she loves to watch DVDs like* Finding Nemo *or* Lord of the Rings. *With zeal, she goes to the CBeebies and Barbie websites. There is little competition between* Three Little Pigs *and the* Lord of the Rings *trilogy. In Molly's world, her Barbies lead active, dynamic lives and she and her friends can while away hours playing at any and all of these activities. The youngest of three, Molly also likes to enter the teen worlds of text messaging, listening to music and emailing, watching her older brother and sister engage in these activities. Molly is not unlike many other 6-year-olds whose home worlds – whether it is using technologies as simple as drawing a picture or making a three-dimensional object, or going to a favourite website – bear no likeness to their schooling world.*

As literacy teachers, how can we possibly mediate between a print-governed, grapho-phonic model of literacy juxtaposed against a multidimensional, multiliterate, multimodal model of literacy? It is a tough question to answer, but in this book we have paved some ground for you to begin thinking within a New Literacy Studies mindset and to build a framework premised on the actual needs of your students as opposed to models from the past. We need a closer alignment between home and school and we must attend to the disparity in our classrooms.

In the book, we have considered how much the world has changed for us. You may look back to the 1990s and remember how the mobile phone was rare and text messaging unheard of. We did not use email as fluently and the skimming between and among websites, word documents and emails was less prevalent. Texts have become shaped by the new uses they have been put to. Texts exist in the same communicational space (for example, the Web) and can cross domains, through, for example, attachments, in the way they never have before. With the Web, they are constantly revisited and re-mediated – making new texts. We can now go to a website and download text which can be recontextualized into a new text.

What do the literacy skills of tomorrow look like? First, literacy needs to be seen as embedded within a wider communicational landscape of meaning and the flows between different meanings need to be acknowledged. The spaces literacy fills can be considered. What does it mean when our students text their friends on bus journeys? How does a support group for teenagers with a particular illness help them come to terms with that illness? There are virtual spaces, actual spaces and spaces which can flow into one another. In the future, the third space, the in-between space between home and school will be filled with virtual and street practices of the text message, the email and the instant message.

In this book, we have tried to bring these practices into the classroom, and engage with them in relation to the teaching of literacy. We have not focused on existing frameworks, but ask for teachers to think outside the box, and remove themselves from where they have been placed by curriculum regimes. For it is through teaching that change can take place.

We also acknowledge the importance of the local. Your local neighbourhood is embedded with meaning, and carries traces of your living within it. Within local spaces, our embodied identities are transforming and making meanings. We hope that this book celebrates local meanings. Within the global landscape, we also notice how children link to neighbourhoods and their work reflects the limits of the local. In some neighbourhoods, there is little access to other spaces due to poor transport links and low economic status. However, through email, and the Web, children can gain access to global spaces and meanings. The link from local to global flows both ways and we recognize this quality when we watch the flow of texts across local and global sites.

Above all, *literacy is about meaning*. This seems obvious and yet is sometimes lost in the plethora of spelling tests and standardized testing. Children use literacy to make meaning and to explore the constraints and possibilities of their worlds. Literacy offers imagined worlds, and its possibilities are endless. Meanings, however, are inscribed within practices, and these practices shape meanings and identities. It is these we celebrate when we talk about literacy practices. In this book, we have celebrated the culture of the ordinary, the everyday, and argued that the everyday cultural practices are what our students bring to the classroom. It is time that they were heard.

Afterword

This book is full of vignettes that illustrate the power of literacy instruction to open up identity options for both students and teachers. So let me start with a vignette of my own that illustrates how the 'construction zone' for teacher and student identity formation can become a 'constriction zone' when literacy instruction is conceptualized by researchers and policy-makers as simply an individual cognitive skill to the exclusion of human relationships and the negotiation of identities.

Shortly after the passage of the No Child Left Behind Act *in the USA, I gave a presentation to several hundred participants at the California Association for Bilingual Education conference in Los Angeles. The presentation focused on literacy instruction for bilingual students. The context of the presentation was the orchestrated discourse in California and elsewhere in the United States that attributed the continuing low academic achievement of bilingual students to both bilingual education and whole-language approaches to literacy instruction. The State of California had mandated several years earlier an approach to reading instruction that was heavily phonics oriented and* No Child Left Behind *was promoting similar approaches.*

In the discussion period following the presentation, the first person who came to the microphone was an elementary school teacher who spoke passionately about the importance of literacy instruction for bilingual children and her extreme frustration at the scripted reading instruction programme that her large urban school district had adopted. The exact implementation of this programme was (in the eyes of the district) supported by coaches or (in the eyes of many teachers) enforced by 'police' who could enter any classroom without warning to check that the programme was being implemented appropriately.

▶

> As she spoke about how she was positioned by this scripted programme and how it affected her capacity to relate in a warm and caring way to her students, this teacher broke down in tears. She did not use these words, but essentially what she was saying was that the script constituted a straitjacket that cut her off from everything she knew, felt and valued about teaching. Her role as teacher was reduced simply to reading the script. Before, reading instruction was an opportunity to generate excitement about books, to engage students in meaning-making in two languages, and to relate at a personal level to them and their families. By contrast, within the regime of truth of the scripted programme, human relationships were 'off-task'.

Literacy and Education is an important book because it articulates in a vividly clear manner a counter-discourse to the assumptions about literacy instruction, illustrated in the vignette above, that currently dominate policy and practice in many countries. Within the USA, these assumptions are presented as 'scientifically proven' (a phrase that occurs frequently on US government websites associated with *No Child Left Behind*). Kate Pahl and Jennifer Rowsell explicitly position their book in opposition to the phonics-oriented drill and skills-based conception of literacy instruction embodied in the *No Child Left Behind* Act in the USA and, to a somewhat lesser extent, the *National Literacy Strategy* in the UK. They argue that the conception of literacy articulated within the New Literacy Studies can generate instructional approaches that enable students to access literacy skills more powerfully than in traditional instructional models. We shall consider the 'scientific' evidence for this claim shortly but, first, let us examine the significance of this book in relation to its theoretical origins and the broader policy context. Of central importance in this regard is the insistence of the authors that identity is inscribed in all aspects of literacy practices.

THE CENTRALITY OF IDENTITY INVESTMENT

The claim that personal identities intersect with literacy practices is unlikely to be controversial to anyone who has observed human behaviour for more than five minutes. We invest our time, energy, intellect and imagination in literacy practices that are meaningful to us in relation to our life goals and personal interests. Many school dropouts with apparently low levels of traditional literacy skills have no difficulty reading baseball or basketball statistics or navigating complex videogames. They are also highly capable of discussing issues related to these spheres of engagement in articulate and critical ways. We all invest our identities minimally in some spheres of literacy practice while in others the investment of identity is enormous.

The centrality of identity investment in literacy development can be seen in typical statistics of school success and failure. In Ontario, for example, 50 per cent of high school students in the Applied (non-academic) programme fail the grade 10 literacy test mandated by the province. As many studies of school failure at the high school level have illustrated, these students' mastery of traditional literacy skills is weak not because they lack the basic cognitive abilities to become literate but because the literacy instruction they experienced throughout their schooling failed to ignite any significant degree of identity investment in school-based literacy. Often, as Pahl and Rowsell point out, these same students manifest highly developed literacies in domains outside the school in which they have chosen to invest their identities. In other words, too often in our schools literacy instruction fails to engage students' cognitive power or their personal interests.

The vignettes, case studies and evaluative research discussed in this volume provide a vividly clear picture of the instructional conditions and literacy practices that invite students' identities into the process of making meaning and generating knowledge. Pahl and Rowsell illustrate how children use a range of tools – from pencils to web page design – to create artefacts that embody their identities and quietly proclaim the intelligence, imagination and talent of their authors. Identity investment is not achieved at the expense of cognitive engagement. On the contrary, the creation of what we have called *identity texts* (Cummins, 2004; Skourtou et al., in press) engages students both cognitively and personally to a far greater degree than traditional transmission-oriented instruction.

THE RADICAL NATURE OF LITERACY AND EDUCATION

The authors of this book may not realize just how radical it is. It threatens the established power structure in education in two ways. First, it shows that ordinary teachers working with ordinary students can create extraordinarily powerful learning opportunities when they step outside the frame of top-down one-size-fits-all mandates and connect imaginatively at a *personal* level with students and communities. Imagination is probably the greatest threat to established social orders, which is perhaps one of the major reasons why its use is rarely encouraged on the part of either teachers or students. The imaginative instructional interactions that leap from the pages of this book are nowhere to be found in the narrow range of skills-based programmes that conform to the 'scientifically-proven' criteria of the *No Child Left Behind* legislation in the USA. Some other contexts afford greater possibilities for innovative literacy instruction than is currently the case in the USA, but in the vast majority, reading and writing are still conceived as skills that are developed within the heads of individual children.

This book invites educators to reclaim the interpersonal space that they orchestrate with their students in the classroom. To reclaim this interpersonal space requires that we recognize that we do have *choices* in how we construct our own identities as educators and that we take responsibility for the instructional choices we make. Thus the book inspires educators to resist coercive top-down mandates that constrict their identity options as educators and violate fundamental principles of how people learn.

The second sense in which this book is radical is that it is one of the first, and certainly the most lucid, expositions of New Literacy Studies to prioritize the voices of teachers and students at least as much as the voices of theorists and researchers. Despite the fact that there is an expanding discourse community within academia concerned with New Literacy Studies, this discourse community has been virtually invisible and inaudible in the public policy sphere as literacy policies in the USA and the UK (as well as in other countries) have jerked sharply backwards towards transmission models of teaching. There have been notable attempts (for example, Newfield and Stein, 2000; Luke, 2002) to inject insights from New Literacy Studies into school curricula but these have been few and far between. Several factors have contributed to the marginalization of New Literacy Studies in recent literacy policy decisions. These include:

- the lack of a coherent body of practice illustrating the application of New Literacy principles;

- the absence of coherent links between classroom practice and the abstract theoretical constructs that form the core of New Literacy theories;

- the implicit assumption that the trajectory of influence goes from theory to practice rather than from practice to theory; ideally, there should be a dialogical relationship between practice and theory (Cummins, 2000) but that has been slow to emerge in the area of New Literacy Studies.

This book addresses all three of these factors which have limited the policy impact of New Literacy Studies. We see a wide range of literacy practices in action and hear the voices of teachers, students and communities as they reflect on these practices. Abstract theoretical constructs (for example, the construct of design in multiliteracies pedagogy [New London Group,

1996]) come alive as they are discussed in relation to concrete innovative literacy practices. Finally, the book sets the stage for a genuine dialogue between practice and theory where literacy practices, and the educators who implement them, contribute actively to the generation of knowledge (theory) rather than simply implementing prior theoretical constructs.

Thus, the book is radical because it is not nearly as easy for policy-makers to ignore as some of the more abstract theoretical accounts of New Literacy Studies. Educators who read this book will immediately recognize the instructional power of the approaches described. They will also recognize that these approaches are not in opposition to the explicit teaching of certain features of literacy (for example, basic phonics, comprehension strategies, and so on). The relevance of clearly explaining 'the rules of the game' is articulated by the New London Group's emphasis on the centrality of *overt instruction* in its version of multiliteracies pedagogy. However, whereas traditional literacy instruction often begins and ends with overt instruction (with occasional *situated practice*), the approaches to literacy instruction articulated in this book take students and teachers into the realms of *critical framing* and *transformed practice*. Suddenly issues of societal power relations are no longer out of bounds within the classroom. The established pedagogical order has long kept critical inquiry into experience, identity, community and power at a safe distance from impressionable and fragile young minds. James Moffett expressed this point 15 years ago:

> *Literacy is dangerous and has always been so regarded ... [W]e feel profoundly ambiguous about literacy. Looking at it as a means of transmitting our culture to our children, we give it priority in education, but recognizing the threat of its backfiring we make it so tiresome and personally unrewarding that youngsters won't want to do it on their own, which is of course when it becomes dangerous ... The net effect of this ambivalence is to give literacy with one hand and take it back with the other, in keeping with our contradictory wish for youngsters to learn to think but only about what we already have in mind for them.* (Moffett, 1989: 85)

Literacy and Education illustrates vividly how power can be created in the interactions between educators and students. By showing so clearly what ordinary teachers working with ordinary students can achieve, it challenges the pedagogical divide that continues to consign low-income students to passive modes of learning while their more affluent peers are stimulated to engage in higher-order thinking and active modes of learning. If the pedagogical directions articulated in this book were implemented in literacy instruction, intellectual power and critical literacy would be within the reach of all students, regardless of linguistic, cultural or class background.

CLASH OF PARADIGMS: THE GEE/SNOW DEBATE

It is not difficult to predict how policy-makers and researchers who align themselves with autonomous conceptions of literacy as primarily an individual cognitive skill will respond to the claims articulated in this book. They will scoff at case studies and vignettes of practice, dismiss the voices of educators and students as irrelevant, and demand 'scientific' evidence, by which they mean experimental and quasi-experimental research. As Allan Luke (2002) has already noted, this clash of paradigms was on display some years ago in a sharp exchange between Catherine Snow and James Paul Gee in the *Journal of Literacy Research*. It is worth revisiting this exchange to examine the nature of the scientific evidence that can be invoked to support expanded conceptions of literacy instruction of the kind articulated in this book.

The debate between Gee and Snow was occasioned by a critical review written by Gee (1999) of the National Research Council report edited by Snow et al. (1998) entitled *Preventing Reading Difficulties in Young Children*. Gee's main points were that the social dimensions of reading were largely ignored in the report and, in particular, the role of poverty as a contributor to reading difficulties was minimally addressed. He pointed out that broader indices of language development that reflected socio-economic background were just as strongly related to reading achievement as phonological awareness which the report focused on as a critical variable. Underlying the problems with the report, he argued, was a conception of reading as a process that happened exclusively within the heads of individuals rather than as a social practice intimately dependent on context.

Snow responded with a vehement attack on New Literacy Studies, arguing that 'If Gee really wishes to promote the impact of the New Literacies approach, he would do well to invest his time in conducting the sort of empirical research that proponents of phonological awareness have produced, rather than simply arguing for his position as the politically and morally correct one' (Snow, 2000: 116). She denied that social realities were ignored in the report and defended the emphasis on the cognitive sub-skills involved with literacy development on the grounds that instruction could address these effectively whereas schools were relatively impotent to change the social conditions of learners.

Gee responded that New Literacies theorists view skills 'as ways of participating in culturally, historically, and institutionally situated social practices, not just as internal cognitive states manifested in behavior'. In this sense, skills are not fixed but change according to the social context and students' modes of participation in these contexts. He elaborated that *the New Literacy Studies is interested not primarily, as is Professor Snow, in 'how cognitive changes within individuals affect their nature of participation,' but in how changes in the nature of participation affect cognition, socially situated identities, and the assessments made about individuals (a basically Vygotskian perspective taken in a sociocultural and sociopolitical direction).* (Gee, 2000: 126)

He suggested that if this social perspective had been given greater weight, a very different report would have emerged with dramatically different policy implications.

A central issue here is the nature of the empirical support that is available to support or refute the claims deriving from these opposing paradigms. Snow suggested that New Literacy theorists will not be credible until they back up their claims with empirical research, implying that no research exists to support the claims of New Literacy Studies. It seems to me that there is ample empirical research to support Gee's main point that the nature of students' engagement with literacy and their literacy 'performance' is strongly influenced by the human relationships or opportunities for social participation existing in any particular situation (inside or outside the classroom) (see Cummins, 2001, for a review). We have seen this in our own recent work exploring multiliteracies pedagogy (Cummins, 2004) and it is very evident in the examples discussed throughout this book. Empirical support for Gee's claim (which is within the mainstream of Vygotskian theory) requires only that researchers demonstrate that changes in students' opportunities for social participation in literacy practices *can* result in different and improved modes of literacy performance. One case study is sufficient to demonstrate this relationship. Demonstration that 'X' *has* occurred automatically proves that 'X' *can* occur. Of course, many more research studies of various kinds may be required to explicate the optimal conditions for maximizing cognitive engagement and identity investment in various kinds of literacy practices.

The dangers of a fundamentalist approach to research and theory development are not confined only to those who espouse positivistic research traditions. New Literacy theorists also need to guard against an *either-or* approach. Highlighting the social dimensions of cognition does not invalidate a research focus on what may be happening inside the heads of individuals, nor does it suggest that a New Literacies perspective is the best or only way to address all questions of literacy development. There are many important questions and research studies associated with literacy development that owe little to New Literacy Studies but have played a central role in policy discussions. Research studies on how long it typically takes English language learners to catch up to grade norms in English academic proficiency (Cummins, 1981; Thomas and Collier, 2002) have, within the context of the research, focused on literacy as an autonomous skill measured by standardized tests but have nevertheless contributed in substantial ways to promoting equity in schooling for bilingual students. Thus, the *either-or* perspective that was evident in the Gee/Snow debate is unhelpful, and fundamentalist approaches to truth and validity are scientifically retrograde regardless of which ideological tradition they represent.

As Gee (2000) points out, the research paradigm reflected in reports such as Snow et al. (1998) and the National Reading Panel (2002) is not just a matter of academic preference or orientation. Because the theoretical frame of these reports was narrowly focused on individual cognition (albeit not denying the relevance of the social), these reports have contributed to the emergence and enforcement of a framework for literacy instruction that is highly transmission oriented and constricts teacher and student identities in classroom interactions. Furthermore, the orientation to literacy instruction that has been enforced and justified as 'scientifically proven' clearly violates the scientific consensus from cognitive psychology regarding how people learn. Ironically, the literacy practices described in the present volume are much more consistent with the cognitive science literature than those described in the vignette that began this Afterword.

HOW PEOPLE LEARN

The research data relating to *How People Learn* was synthesized in a volume with that title published by the National Research Council in the USA (Bransford et al., 2000). That volume represents a significant consensus among cognitive psychologists in relation to how learning occurs and the optimal conditions to foster learning. The authors emphasize the following conditions for effective learning:

- *Learning with deep understanding*. Knowledge is more than just the ability to remember; deeper levels of understanding are required to transfer knowledge from one context to another. This implies that instruction for deep understanding involves the development of critical literacy (reading between the lines) rather than simply literal or surface comprehension of text.

- *Building on pre-existing knowledge*. Prior knowledge, skills, beliefs and concepts significantly influence what learners notice about their environment and how they organize and interpret it. This principle implies that in classrooms with students from culturally and linguistically diverse backgrounds, instruction must explicitly activate students' prior knowledge and build relevant background knowledge as necessary. The implied acknowledgement and affirmation of students' language and cultural backgrounds is not socio-politically neutral. Rather, it explicitly challenges the omission and subordination of students' culture and language within typical one-size-fits-all transmission-oriented classrooms.

■ *Promoting active learning.* Learners should be supported in taking control of, and self-regulating, their own learning. When students take ownership of the learning process and invest their identities in the outcomes of learning, the resulting understanding will be deeper than when learning is passive.

■ *Support within the community of learners.* Learning takes place in a social context and a supportive learning community encourages dialogue, apprenticeship and mentoring. Learning is not simply a cognitive process that takes place inside the heads of individual students; it also involves socialization into particular communities of practice. Within these learning communities novices are enabled to participate in the practices of the community from the very beginning of their involvement. The learning community can include the classroom, the school, the family and broader community, and virtual communities enabled through electronic communication.

Bransford et al. do not use terms such as 'critical literacy' or 'identity invest-ment' but these constructs are certainly consistent with the overall orientation of the learning principles they articulate. These principles specify some minimal requirements for effective learning. They also bring into immediate focus the lack of scientific credibility of approaches that rely on simple transmission of knowledge and skills from teachers to learners. Exclusive reliance on transmission pedagogy is likely to entail memorization rather than learning for deep understanding, minimal activation of students' prior knowledge, and passive rather than active learning. The social supports for learning within communities of learners are likewise absent from trans-mission approaches. Thus, the scripted literacy instruction touted as 'scientifically proven' and inflicted on low-income students in urban class-rooms is diametrically opposed to the scientific consensus regarding how people learn. The uncritical adoption of a behaviourist literacy agenda on the basis of a highly flawed and narrowly focused interpretation of the empirical research has effectively denied low-income and bilingual students access to participation in empowering literacy practices, at least within the school context.

MULTILITERACIES PEDAGOGY REVISITED

As noted above, until the arrival of this inspiring book, New Literacies Studies have tended to be top-heavy theoretically, with little 'talkback' from classroom instruction to theory. One approach to generating theory from practice is to examine the images of children, teachers and society that are implied in powerful forms of literacy instruction, such as those described in the preceding chapters. Colleagues and I have been engaged in attempting to do just this in the context of a collaborative Canada-wide project entitled *From Literacy to Multiliteracies: Designing Learning Environments for Knowledge Generation within the New Economy* (Early et al., 2002).

A radically different image of the child is implied in the classrooms we have observed than in more typical transmission-oriented classrooms. Within the framework of multiliteracies pedagogy, broadly defined, educators construct and shape an image of the child into reality through the classroom interactions they orchestrate. Our observations allow us to articulate in a very concrete way five central components of a multiliteracies pedagogy that prioritizes the role of identity investment in learning:

- Multiliteracies pedagogy constructs an image of the child as intelligent, imaginative and linguistically talented; individual differences in these traits do not diminish the potential of each child to shine in specific ways.

- Multiliteracies pedagogy acknowledges and builds on the cultural and linguistic capital (prior knowledge/funds of knowledge) of students and communities.

- Multiliteracies pedagogy aims explicitly to promote cognitive engagement and identity investment on the part of students.

- Multiliteracies pedagogy enables students to construct knowledge, create literature and art, and act on social realities through dialogue and critical inquiry.

- Multiliteracies pedagogy employs a variety of technological tools to support students' construction of knowledge, literature and art and their presentation of this intellectual work to multiple audiences through the creation of identity texts.

Identity texts refer to products of students' creative work or performances carried out within the interpersonal space orchestrated by teacher–student interactions. Students invest their identities in these texts (written, spoken, visual, musical, dramatic or combinations in multimodal form) that then hold up a mirror to students in which their identities are reflected back in a positive light. When students share identity texts with multiple audiences (peers, teachers, parents, grandparents, sister classes, the media, and so on) they are likely to receive positive feedback and affirmation of self in inter-action with these audiences. Although not always an essential component, technology acts as an amplifier to enhance the process of identity invest-ment and affirmation. It facilitates the production of these texts, makes them look more accomplished and expands the audiences and potential for affirmative feedback.

The emerging principles of multiliteracies pedagogy articulated above are clearly compatible with those of the New London Group (1996) but they differ in so far as they emerged as much from practice as from theory and they highlight the centrality of identity investment that is implied but not made explicit in the New London Group framework. The principles are also expressed in such a way that their consistency with Bransford et al.'s description of how people learn is evident. I would invite readers to bring these principles into dialogue with the lit-eracy practices described in *Literacy and Education* and assess to what extent they adequately capture important underlying dimensions of these practices. Where gaps exist, the practices described in this volume can inform the emerging theoretical framework.

In conclusion, I would like to express my appreciation to Kate Pahl and Jennifer Rowsell for their invitation to be part of the dialogue that this book represents. There are also images of the child, of the teacher and of society inscribed in the pages of this book. These images are full of possi-bilities that we can only imagine. And surely that is the point. As Kieran Egan and Dan Nadaner argued some years ago: 'imagination … is at the heart of any truly educational experience … Stimulating the imagination is not an alternative educational activity to be argued for in competition with other claims; it is a prerequisite to making any activity educational' (1988: ix). Reading this wonderful book was for me very much an educa-tional experience precisely because it stimulated my imagination in relation to what schools and educators *can* achieve in enabling ordinary students to generate new knowledge, create literature and art, and act on social realities.

Jim Cummins
University of Toronto
October 2004

REFERENCES

Bransford, J.D., Brown, A.L. and Cocking, R.R. (2000) *How People Learn: Brain, Mind, Experience, and School*. Washington, DC: National Academy Press.

Cummins, J. (1981) 'Age on arrival and immigrant second language learning in Canada: a Reassessment', *Applied Linguistics*, 1: 132–49.

Cummins, J. (2000) *Language, Power, and Pedagogy: Bilingual Children in the Crossfire*. Clevedon: Multilingual Matters.

Cummins, J. (2001) *Negotiating Identities: Education for Empowerment in a Diverse Society*. 2nd edn. Los Angeles, CA: California Association for Bilingual Education.

Cummins, J. (2004) 'Multiliteracies pedagogy and the role of identity texts,' in K. Leithwood, P. McAdie, N. Bascia, and A. Rodigue (eds), *Teaching for deep understanding: Towards the Ontario curriculum that we need.* (pp. 68–74). Toronto: Ontario Institute for Studies in Education of the University of Toronto and the Elementary Teachers Federation of Ontario.

Early, M. et al. (2002) *From Literacy to Multiliteracies: Designing Learning Environments for Knowledge Generation within the New Economy*. Proposal funded by the Social Sciences and Humanities Research Council of Canada.

Egan, K. and Nadaner, D. (eds) (1988) *Imagination and Education*. New York: Teachers College Press.

Gee, J.P. (1999) 'Reading and the new literacy studies: reframing the National Academy of Sciences report on reading', *Journal of Literacy Research*, 31: 355–74.

Gee, J.P. (2000) 'The limits of reframing: a response to Professor Snow', *Journal of Literacy Research*, 32: 121–30.

Luke, A. (2002) 'What happens to literacies old and new when they're turned into policy?', in D.E. Alverman (ed.), *Adolescents and Literacies in a Digital World*. New York: Peter Lang. pp. 186–203.

Moffett, J. (1989) 'Censorship and spiritual education' *English Education*, 21: 70–87.

National Reading Panel. (2000) *Teaching Children to Read: An Evidence-Based Assessment of the Scientific Research Literature on Reading and its Implications for Reading Instruction*. Washington, DC: NICHD.

New London Group (1996) 'A pedagogy of multiliteracies: designing social futures', *Harvard Educational Review*, 66: 60–92.

Newfield, D. and Stein, P. (2000) 'The multiliteracies project: South African teachers respond', in B. Cope and M. Kalantzis (eds), *Multiliteracies: Literacy Learning and Design of Social Futures*. London: Routledge. pp. 292–310.

Skourtou, E., Kourtis-Kazoullis, V. and Cummins, J. (in press) 'Designing virtual learning environments for academic language development', in J. Weiss, J. Nolan and V. Nincic (eds), *Handbook of Virtual Learning*. Dordrecht: Kluwer Academic.

Snow, C.E. (2000) 'On the limits of reframing: rereading the National Academy of Sciences report on reading', *Journal of Literacy Research*, 32: 113–20.

Snow, C.E., Burns, M.S. and Griffin, P. (eds) (1998) *Preventing Reading Difficulties in Young Children*. Washington, DC: National Academy Press.

Thomas, W.P. and Collier, V.P. (2002) *A National Study of School Effectiveness for Language Minority Students' Long-Term Academic Achievement*. Santa Cruz, CA: Center for Research on Education, Diversity and Excellence, University of California-Santa Cruz. Available at http//www.crede.ucsc.edu

Glossary of Terms

Affordance Choosing materials appropriately for the task, for example choosing a font for a poster which carries effect.

Artefact An object that is tied to a context and an identity. It carries a story and has a past. For example, framed photographs.

Autonomous A model of literacy independent of social context. Literacy as a set of skills. For example, phonics programmes, reading schemes.

Avatars Characters that are used to navigate electronic texts, for example, Harry Potter in the computer game *Harry Potter*.

Bilingual Being able to speak two languages, for example Urdu and Gujurati.

Communicational landscape The different ways people make meaning, in either visual or verbal forms. For example, the Internet offers a vast array of communicational sites.

Communities of practice Groups of people with common beliefs, values, ways of speaking and being. We all belong to a number of them, for example, home, school, office and so on.

Constraint The things that stop texts being functional, for example texts that are too linguistic for pre-school children.

Critical literacy A way of looking at the embodied understandings within texts as opposed to a surface reading of texts. Seeing power within texts. For example, differentiating between two newspapers, such as the *Observer* and the *Daily Mail*.

Crossing Moving from one site to the next, for example, from home to school.

Cultural capital The currency we bring to situations, for example, children bring experiences from home to school.

Cultural practices The things we do with culture, the actions that take place around culture and the re-fashioning of culture in texts and artefacts, for example, parents making books with children on the Web.

Cultural resources A way of recognizing what children bring to educational settings from their own cultural heritage, for example, bringing in new information to school about cultural events.

Culture A way of describing a characteristic of human life by which people share values, behaviours, ways of speaking, ways of being, for example, football in the UK.

Dialogic A give and take situation, a type of discourse, a way of speaking, for example, an interview in a magazine.

discourse Language in a social context, for example, the language of Postgraduate Certificate of Education students.

Discourse Language and other stuff, for example, gestures, clothes, for example, bikers.

Discursive identity The way we speak is tied to who we are, our identity in the world. For example, when we become a teacher we take on a specific discursive identity around teaching as opposed to, for example, mothering.

Domains Domains are spaces or worlds where we use literacy, for example, work, home and school.

Ethnography The study of cultural identities and worlds, which focuses on ways of recording those cultural identities, and standing away and drawing close to the experience.

Family literacy Any activity which involves parents and children in literacy. Often taught in school settings, with joint programmes for parents and children to enjoy.

Figured worlds Collectively realized 'as-if' worlds that we inhabit. Figured worlds are opened up by artefacts. For example, a staffroom in a school is a figured world.

Funds of knowledge The cultural resources that families and homes bring to other settings. For example, home stories brought to classrooms.

Genre theory The medium, the objects, and the manner or mode of presentation that best fits the work. For example, a formal letter with letterhead and with a particular language is a genre.

Global Networks and entities that exist outside of the local. For example, the Internet is a global network.

Global literacies Literacy practices that are associated with globalization. For example, the language used within global banking institutions like Lloyds Bank.

Globalization The process of imposed networks and entities into local domains. For example, McDonald's in local domains.

Hybridity Different cultural forms interacting in the same space. For example, two children in a playground incorporating North American English with Chinese.

Identity A way of describing a sense of self that is in practice. For example, two literacy teachers chatting at a language and literacy conference.

Identity-in-practice Identities as expressed in artefacts, texts, and discourse. For example, your diary is an expression of your identity-in-practice.

Ideology/ideological Any system of cultural meaning which is infused with power that seeps into practices and texts. For example, a newspaper with a liberal slant on issues.

Intercultural communication Communication between cultures that informs practice. For example, using children's funds of knowledge in the classroom.

Literacies Ways of expressing meaning in linguistic forms across domains. For example, text messaging.

Literacy Ways of making meaning with linguistic stuff in a communicative landscape. For example, early writing with a drawing.

Literacy event Any action involving the comprehension of print. For example, writing a lesson plan.

Literacy of fusion It is combining elements of linguistic and visual in order to create a text. For example, using PowerPoint for a presentation.

Literacy practice Patterns of activity around literacy. For example, a guided reading session with a particular set of practices.

Local The sense of place and neighbourhood that people inhabit. For example, community centres.

Macro Activity at a strategic level (for example, government). For example, *No Child Left Behind*.

Materiality The stuff we use to make texts. For example, tissue paper to make a collage.

Meso Activity at an intermediate level (for example, school policy document). For example, home–school reading policy.

Micro Activity at a local level (for example, teachers in classrooms). For example, a year 5 teacher working with a student.

Mode Making meaning from lots of different stuff. For example, graphic interface using web-based resources.

Motivated sign Infusing our identity into texts. For example, a child putting a particular colour of paint in a drawing.

Multilingual literacies Different linguistic identities can be employed in the same space. For example, Arabic language practices functioning alongside English language practices.

Multilingual The employment of different linguistic identities in a particular space. For example, Punjabi, Urdu and English used in a home space.

Multiliteracies Using different linguistic systems within the same space. For example, home–school book-making using different languages and dual texts.

Multimodality A way of making meaning that allows for different modes. For example, model-making as a form of communication.

Multimodal literacy Literacy teaching and learning that takes account of *all* modes within texts of all kinds.

Multiple literacies Different linguistic systems working within the same space. For example, Chinese, Turkish and English students working on a language activity at a writing centre.

Narrative The showing or the telling of these events and the mode selected for that to take place. For example, a story told in a cartoon strip.

New Literacy Studies An approach to literacy and language learning that looks at how literacy is used in everyday life – from literacy events like guided reading at school, to reading a newspaper in a café.

Out-of-school literacy practices Practices which are not infused with literacy pedagogy. For example, children playing videogames.

Pedagogy The inscribing into practice of teacherly activities. For example, building assessment strands into a unit.

Reader response Being able to identify texts as crafted objects and being alert to the values and interests that texts have within them.

Recontextualization Carrying practices across sites and putting them in a different context. For example, taking popular songs from the radio and inserting them into school discourse.

Ruling passions The way people's interest affects their literacy practices. For example, gardening.

Schooled literacy A notion of literacy practices tied to school learning. For example, homework.

Sign A sign is a combination of meaning and form. For example, a road sign.

Site A place that is specific. For example, a Mosque.

Social practice Cultural patterns and forms inscribed into everyday lives. For example, eating breakfast.

Space A space can be real or imagined. For example, a classroom or a chatroom.

Strategies The way the powerful shape space and practices. For example, standardized assessment tests.

Symbol A sign that refers to an idea. Madeleine's lines for each family member in Chapter 2.

Synaesthesia The blurring of different modes into one another. For example, seeing words as colours.

Syncretic literacy Two different cultural practices merging in one literacy practice. For example, a reading scheme in a different cultural space.

Tactics The ways people who live within institutionalized spaces manipulate them. For example, students who write on desks.

Text An articulation of a discourse. For example, a website for a clothing company.

Texts as artefacts Texts that have a history or story of their making. For example, a photograph album.

Third space It is a space where students draw on different discourses that are in-between other domains.

Traces It is an inscription to access a history. For example, a novel carries traces of an author's experience and ideas.

Visual Communication Ways of expressing meaning in the visual. For example, television.

Weblogs Identity-infused web spaces with personal messages and artefacts.

References

Alvermann, D. (2002) *Adolescents and Literacies in a Digital World*. New York: Peter Lang.

Bartlett, L. and Holland, D. (2002) 'Theorizing the space of literacy practices', *Ways of Knowing*, 2 (1): 10–22.

Barton, D. and Hamilton, M. (1998) *Local Literacies: Reading and Writing in One Community*. London: Routledge.

Barton, D. and Hamilton, M. (2000) 'Literacy practices', in D. Barton, M. Hamilton and R. Ivanic (eds), *Situated Literacies: Reading and Writing in Context*. London: Routledge, pp. 7–15.

Barton, D., Hamilton, M. and Ivanic, R. (eds) (2000) *Situated Literacies: Reading and Writing in Context*. London: Routledge.

Bearne, E. (2003) 'Rethinking literacy; communication, representation and text', *Reading: Literacy and Language*, 37 (3): 98–103.

Bianco, J.L. (2000) 'Multiliteracies and multilingualism', in B. Cope and M. Kalantzis (eds), *Multiliteracies: Literacy Learning and the Design of Social Futures*. London: Routledge, pp. 92–105.

Blackledge, A. (2000) 'Power relations and the social construction of "literacy" and "illiteracy": the experience of Bangladeshi women in Birmingham', in M. Martin-Jones and K. Jones (eds), *Multilingual Literacies: Reading and Writing Different Worlds*. Amsterdam: John Benjamins, pp. 37–54.

Bourdieu, P. (1991) *Language and Symbolic Power*. London: Polity Press.

Brandt, D. and Clinton, K. (2002) 'The limits of the local: expanding perspectives of literacy as a social practice', *Journal of Literacy Research*, 34 (3): 337–56.

Brooks, G., Gorman, T., Harman, D. and Wilkin, A. (1996) *Family Literacy Works*. London: BSA.

Burnett, C. and Myers, J. (2002) ' "Beyond the Frame": exploring children's literacy practices', *Reading: Literacy and Language*, 36 (2): 56–62.

Carrington, V. and Luke, A. (2003) 'Reading, homes, and families: from postmodern to modern?', in A. van Kleeck, S. Stahl and E. Bauer (eds), *On Reading Books to Children: Parents and Teachers*, London: Lawrence Erlbaum Associates, pp. 231–52.

Clay, M. (1975) *What Did I Write? Beginning Writing Behaviour*. London: Heinemann.

Condelli, L. (2003) 'Effective instruction for adult ESOL literacy students: findings from the What Works study', paper given at the first NRDC International Conference, Nottingham, March.

Cope, B. and Kalantzis, M. (eds) (2000) *Multiliteracies: Literacy Learning and the Design of Social Futures*. London: Routledge.

Cope, B. and Kalantzis M. (n.d.) *Putting Multiliteracies to the Test*. www.alea.edu.au/multilit.htm (accessed 29 April 2004).

Cummins, J. (2001) *Negotiating Identities: Education for Empowerment in a Diverse Society*, 2nd edn. Los Angeles, CA: California for Bilingual Education.

Cummins, J. (2002) 'Deconstructing the "Literacy Crisis" ', in M. Kalantzis, G. Varnava and B. Cope (eds), *Learning For the Future: New Worlds, New Literacies, New People*. Australia: Common Ground Publishing, pp.109–29.

De Certeau, M. (1984) *The Practice of Everyday Life*. trans. Steven Rendell. Berkeley, CA: University of California Press.

Department for Education and Employment (DfEE) (1998) *The National Literacy Strategy Framework for Teaching*.

Duranti, A. and Ochs, E. (1996) 'Syncretic literacy: multiculturalism in Samoan American families', National Center for Research on Cultural Diversity and Second Language Learning' *Research Report No. 16*, University of California, Santa Cruz.

Dyson, A.H. (2003) *The Brothers and Sisters Learn to Write: Popular Literacies in Childhood and School Cultures*. New York: Teachers College Press.

Engeström, Y. (1999) 'Activity theory and individual and social transformation', in Y. Engeström, R. Miettinen and R.L. Punamäki (eds), *Perspectives on Activity Theory*. Cambridge: Cambridge University Press, pp. 19–38.

Feiler, A., Johnson, D., Scanlan, M., Greenhough, P., Andrews, J., Yee, W.C. and Hughes, M. (in press) *Linking the Home and School: Primary Literacy*. London: RoutledgeFalmer.

Gee, J.P. (1996) *Social Linguistics and Literacies: Ideology in Discourses*, 2nd edn. London: Taylor and Francis.

Gee, J.P. (1999) *An Introduction to Discourse Analysis: Theory and Method.* London: Routledge.

Gee, J.P. (2003). *What Video Games Have to Teach Us about Learning and Literacy.* New York: Palgrave Macmillan.

Graham, L. (2004) 'Its Spiderman! Popular culture in writing journals in the early years', ESRC Research Seminar Series, Children's Literacy and Popular Culture, University of Sheffield, 2002–04, 11 February 2004, http://www.shef.ac.uk/literacy/ESRC/pdf/papers/LG_11_2.pdf

Gregory, E. (ed.) (1997) *One Child, Many Worlds: Early Learning in Multicultural Communities.* London: David Fulton.

Gregory, E. and Williams, A. (2000) 'Work or play? Unofficial literacies in the lives of two East London communities', in M. Martin-Jones and K. Jones (eds), *Multilingual Literacies: Reading and Writing Different Worlds.* Amsterdam: John Benjamins, pp. 37–54.

Gumperz, J. (1982) *Discourse Strategies.* Cambridge: Cambridge University Press.

Gutiérrez, K.D., Baquedano-Lopez, P., Alvarez, H. and Chiu, M.M. (1999) 'Building a culture of collaboration through hybrid language practices', *Theory into Practice*, 38: 87–93.

Hannon, P. and Nutbrown, C. (1997) 'Teachers' use of a conceptual framework for early literacy education with parents', *Teacher Development*, 1 (3): 405–20.

Hannon, P. and Nutbrown, C. (2001) 'Outcomes for children and parents of an early literacy education parent involvement programme', paper presented at the Annual Conference of the British Educational Research Association, Leeds.

Heath, S.B. (1983) *Ways with Words: Language, Life and Work in Communities and Classrooms.* Cambridge: Cambridge University Press.

Hinchman, K.A., Alvermann, D.E., Boyd, F.B., Brozo, W.G. and Vacca, R.T. (2004) 'Supporting older students' in and out-of-school literacies', *Journal of Adolescent and Adult Literacy*, 47 (4): 304–10.

Holland, D., Lachicotte, W., Skinner, D. and Cain, C. (2001) *Identity and Agency in Cultural Worlds.* Cambridge, MA: Harvard University Press.

Hornberger, N. (2000) 'Multilingual literacies, literacy practices, and the continua of biliteracy', in M. Martin-Jones and K. Jones (eds), *Multilingual Literacies: Reading and Writing Different Worlds.* Amsterdam: John Benjamins, pp. 253–368.

Hull, G. and Schultz, K. (eds) (2002) *School's Out! Bridging Out-of-school Literacies With Classroom Practice.* New York: Teachers College Press.

Hymes, D. (ed.) (1996) *Ethnography, Linguistics, Narrative Inequality: Towards an Understanding of Voice.* London: Routledge.

Janks, H. and Comber, B. (2004) 'Critical literacy across continents', paper presented at the American Educational Research Association, San Diego, 12–18 April.

Jewitt, C. and Kress, G. (eds) (2003) *Multimodal Literacy*. New York: Peter Lang.

Kenner, C. (2000) *Home Pages: Literacy Links for Bilingual Children*. Stoke-on-Trent; Trentham Books.

Knobel, M. and Lankshear, C. (2003) 'Researching young children's out-of-school literacy practices', in N. Hall, J. Larson and J. Marsh (eds), *Handbook of Early Childhood Literacy*. London, New Delhi and Thousand Oaks, CA: Sage, pp. 51–65.

Kress, G. (1997) *Before Writing: Rethinking the Paths to Literacy*. London: Routledge.

Kress, G. (2003). *Literacy in the New Media Age*. London: Routledge.

Kress, G. and Van Leeuwen, T. (1996) *Reading Images: The Grammar of Visual Design*. London: Routledge.

Lankshear, C. and Knobel, M. (2003) *New Literacies: Changing Knowledge and Classroom Learning*. Buckingham and Philadelphia, PA: Open University Press.

Larson, J. and Gatto, L.A. (2004) 'Tactical underlife: understanding students' perceptions', *Journal of Early Childhood Literacy*, 4 (1): 11–42.

Lave, J. and Holland, D. (eds) (2001) *History in Person: Enduring Struggles, Contentious Practice, Intimate Identities*. New Mexico: School of American Research Press.

Luke, A. (2002) 'Literacy, globalisation and curriculum practice', keynote talk given at the UKRA International Conference, Chester, July.

Luke, A. and Carrington, V. (2002) 'Globalisation, literacy, curriculum practice', in R. Fisher, G. Brooks and M. Lewis (eds), *Raising Standards in Literacy*. London: RoutledgeFalmer pp. 231–250

Luke, A. and Luke C. (2000) 'A situated perspective on cultural globalization', in N.C. Burbules and C.A. Torres (eds), *Globalization and Education Critical Perspectives*. London: Routledge, pp. 275–99.

Marsh, J. and Thompson, P. (2001) 'Parental involvement in literacy development: using media texts', *Journal of Research in Reading*, 24 (3): 266–78.

Marsh, J. (2003) 'Early childhood literacy and popular culture', in N. Hall, J. Larson and J. Marsh (eds), *Handbook of Early Childhood Literacy*. London, New Delhi and Thousand Oaks, CA: Sage, pp. 112–25.

Mathewman, S., with Blight, A. and Davies, C. (2004) 'What does multimodality mean for English? Creative tensions in teaching new texts and new literacies', http://www.interactiveeducation.ac.uk/out_mat.pdf (accessed 29 April 2004).

McDonald, L. (2004) 'Moving from reader response to critical reading: developing 10–11 year olds' ability as analytical readers of texts', *Literacy*, 38 (1): 17–25.

McLuhan, M. (1964) *Understanding Media: The Extensions of Man.* London: Routledge.

Meacham, S.J. (2004). 'Hip-hop literacy: critical crossroads, alternative systems, and the plantation-project-prison continuum in hip-hop lyricism', presentation ESRC conference on Children's Popular Culture and Literacy, Sheffield, 20 March.

Michaels, S. (1986) 'Narrative presentations: an oral preparation for literacy with first graders', in J. Cook-Gumperz (ed.), *The Social Construction of Literacy.* Cambridge: Cambridge University Press, pp. 94–116.

Millard, E. (2003) 'Towards a literacy of fusion: new times, new teaching and learning?', *Reading: Literacy and Language*, 37 (1): 3–9.

Moll, L., Amanti, C., Neff, D. and Gonzalez, N. (1992) 'Funds of knowledge for teaching: using a qualitative approach to connect homes and classrooms', *Theory into Practice*, 31 (2): 132–41.

Moje, E.B., Ciechanowski, K.M., Kramer, K., Ellis, L., Carrillo, R. and Collazo, T. (2004) 'Working toward third space in content area literacy: an examination of everyday funds of knowledge and discourse', *Reading Research Quarterly*, 39 (1): 38–70.

Moss, G. (1999) 'Texts in contexts: mapping out the gender differentiation of the reading curriculum', *Pedagogy, Culture and Society*, 7 (3): 507–22.

Moss, G. (2003) 'Putting the text back into practice: junior-age non-fiction as objects of design', in C. Jewitt and G. Kress (eds), *Multimodal Literacy.* London: Peter Lang, pp. 73–87.

Newfield, D. and Stein, P. (2000) 'The Multiliteracies Project: South African teachers respond', in B. Cope, and M. Kalantzis (eds), *Multiliteracies: Literacy Learning and the Design of Social Futures.* London: Routledge, pp. 292–310.

Nixon, J., Allan, J. and Mannion, G. (2001) 'Educational renewal as democratic practice: "new" community schooling in Scotland', *International Journal of Inclusive Education*, 5 (4): 329–52.

No Child Left Behind (2002) Washington, DC: US Department of Education.

Pahl, K. (1999) *Transformations: Making Meaning in Nursery Education.* London: Trentham Books.

Pahl, K. (2002) 'Ephemera, mess and miscellaneous piles: texts and practices in families', *Journal of Early Childhood Literacy*, 2 (2): 145–65.

Pahl, K. (2003) 'Children's text making at home: transforming meaning across modes', in C. Jewitt, and G. Kress (eds), *Multimodal Literacy*. New York: Peter Lang, pp. 139–54.

Pahl, K. (2004a) *All these Umbrellas under One Canopy: An Evaluation of Read on Write Away! Family Learning, Derbyshire*. Matlock: Read On Write Away!

Pahl, K. (2004b) *Making Space for Learning*. Croydon: University of Sheffield, Croydon CETS.

Pahl, K. (2005) 'Narrative spaces and multiple identities: children's textual explorations of console games in home settings', in J. Marsh (ed.), *Popular Culture, New Media and Digital Literacy in Early Childhood*. London: RoutledgeFalmer.

Purcell-Gates, V., Degener, S.C., Jacobson, E. and Soler, M. (2002) 'Impact of authentic adult literacy instruction on adult literacy practices', *Reading Research Quarterly*, 37 (1): 70–92.

Qualifications and Curriculum Authority (QCA) (2004) *More than Words: Multimodal Texts in the Classroom*. London: UKLA/QCA.

Rampton, M.B.H. (1992) 'Scope for empowerment in sociolinguistics?', in D. Cameron, E. Frazer, P. Harvey, M.B.H. Rampton and K. Richardson (eds), *Researching Language: Issues of Power and Method*. London: Routledge, pp. 29–64.

Rashid, N. and Gregory, E. (1997) 'Learning to read, reading to learn: the importance of siblings in the language development of young bilingual children', in E. Gregory (ed.), *One Child, Many Worlds: Early Learning in Multicultural Communities*. London: David Fulton, pp. 107–22.

Rogers, R. (2003) *A Critical Discourse Analysis of Family Literacy Practices: Power in and out of Print*. Hillsdale, NJ: Lawrence Erlbaum Associates.

Rowsell, J. (2000). 'Publishing practices in printed education: British and Canadian perspectives on educational publishing'. PhD thesis, University of London.

Saxena, M. (2000) 'Taking account of history and culture in community-based research on multilingual literacy', in M. Martin-Jones and K. Jones (eds), *Multilingual Literacies: Reading and Writing Different Worlds*. Amsterdam: John Benjamins, pp. 275–98.

Schultz, K. (2002) 'Looking across space and time: reconceptualizing literacy learning in and out of school', *Research in the Teaching of English*, 36: 356–90.

Scribner, S. and Cole, M. (1981) *The Psychology of Literacy*. Cambridge: Harvard University Press.

Street, B.V. (1984) *Literacy in Theory and Practice*. Cambridge: Cambridge University Press.

Street, B.V. (ed.) (1993) *Cross-Cultural Approaches to Literacy*. Cambridge: Cambridge University Press.

Street, B.V. and Street, J. (1991) 'The schooling of literacy', in D. Barton and R. Ivanic (eds), *Writing in the Community*. London: Sage, pp. 143–66.

Taylor, D. (1983) *Family Literacy: Young Children Learning to Read and Write*. Portsmouth, NH: Heinemann.

Tizard, B. and Hughes, M. (1984) *Young Children Learning: Talking and Thinking at Home and at School*. London: Fontana.

Volk, D. (1997) 'Continuities and discontinuities: teaching and learning in the home and school of a Puerto Rican five year old', in E. Gregory (ed.), *One Child, Many Worlds: Early Learning in Multicultural Communities*. London: David Fulton, pp. 47–62.

Vygotsky, L. (1978) *Mind in Society: The Development of Higher Psychological Processes*, (eds) M. Cole, V. John-Steiner, S. Scribner and E. Souberman. Cambridge, MA: Harvard University Press.

Wells, G. (1986) *The Meaning Makers: Children Learning Language and Using Language to Learn*. Portsmouth, NH: Heinemann.

Wenger, E. (1998) *Communities of Practice: Learning, Meaning and Identity*. Cambridge: Cambridge University Press.

Williams, R. (2001) (first published 1961) *The Long Revolution*. Hertford: Broadview Press.

Wilson, A. (2000) 'There is no escape from third space theory: borderline discourse and the "in between" literacies of prisons', in D. Barton, M. Hamilton and R. Ivanic, (eds), *Situated Literacies: Reading and Writing in Context*. London: Routledge, pp. 54–69.

Index